GOD CROWNED ME
BEFORE HE CLEANED ME

God Crowned Me Before He Cleaned Me

Chaplain Tammie Holmes

A Memoir of Child Sexual Abuse Trauma
Addiction, Incarceration and Recovery

XULON PRESS

Xulon Press
2301 Lucien Way #415
Maitland, FL 32751
407.339.4217
www.xulonpress.com

Unless otherwise indicated, Scripture quotations taken from the Holy Bible, New Living Translation (NLT). Copyright ©1996, 2004, 2007 by Tyndale House Foundation. Used by permission of Tyndale House Publishers, Inc.

Paperback ISBN-13: 978-1-6628-5644-0
Ebook ISBN-13: 978-1-6628-5645-7

TABLE OF CONTENTS

Foreword

I am the first-born daughter of Chaplain Tammie. Unfortunately, I do not have a lot of memories from my childhood... good or bad. I guess that is just my unconscious mind suppressing the trauma I endured growing up. I do remember the hurt, anger, and disappointment I felt towards my mom, especially as a teenager and young adult. I had to grow up a lot faster than other kids my age. Part of me is thankful, because that forced me to become so strong and independent (almost to a fault). It was not until I was an adult with my own children, that I was able to fully understand what my mom went through as a child and why she may have made the choices she made, that in turn affected her children. At that point, I was able to let go of a lot of that hurt and anger and allow our relationship to grow. I am proud of my mom's accomplishments and the progress she has made to become who she is today. I am grateful that she is still here, and we can have a relationship, even though it may not be the type of mother-daughter relationship

I envisioned or longed for. I have had to accept that it is what it is.

I am Chaplain Tammie's second daughter. I remember my mom leaving for days, forcing me to step up and take care of my sisters because if I did not do it there was no one else to count on. At 15 I got pregnant and was so scared to tell my mom, so when I got the courage to tell her she said she already knew, and babies are a blessing from God. My little boy sure did bless our family and brought so much joy to our lives. Although my mom was an addict, she always made sure we had a clean house and food on the table. At one point in my life my mom and I were so close, but I could never truly let my guard all the way down because I never wanted to feel that hurt again that I felt when I was younger. I never did truly forgive my mom until recently because I could not let go of the hurt, I had in my heart from my childhood. At one point I felt like the stepchild and that hurt came right back from when I was younger, and the feeling is indescribable. I do not even remember my mom telling us she loved us unless we said it first. Dysfunctional is an understatement of what our family was. I can say today that I forgive my mom. I am a mother of four and I strive daily to be the best mom I can be to them. What I want my mom to know is I admire her courage, I understand her hurt, I love her loving heart and I forgive her! Mom no one said life would be easy, but I truly believe it is worth it. You played a major role in the mother I am today. Your mistakes are my treasures...love you mom

———————✳———————

I want to start off saying, I feel so honored that my mom asked me to write this short perspective in her book. I am Chaplain Tammie's 3rd daughter. I know mine and my sister's point of views on how life was growing up will be completely different. Growing up I looked at my mom's addiction as a disease, something she did not want to do but her body would not let her function without drugs. I never looked at my mom as a bad mother, it was our life and her being a functional drug abuser was my norm. Growing up my momma made sure we had a decent place to live, nice clothes to wear and food in our stomach. To be honest my big sisters did an excellent job keeping some things in the dark until I reached about 12 years old. One thing that bothered me growing up about my mom was the company she kept sometimes. I hated all her friends and I promise every one of her friends knew it. I was so rude and disrespectful to them and had no care in the world. My mom never corrected me because she knew those people were no good and I was right with everything I was saying. My mom was never affectionate. I do not know if it was drugs or the sexual abuse she encountered. But as a child I sure did want and need those hugs. My mom has made up for them loss hugs and she tell me she loves me all the time now. To be honest drugs did not take over my mom's character, lol if she was high or sober, she was her same silly self that speaks her mind. I sometimes do wish I had the mom I have today when I was a child, I know I am a good person now, but I would have turned out ten times better. I am the child that has my mom's giving heart and passion for people in need. That one thing that I love that we share and that we have in common. My mom is truly one of my best friends and I admire and respect the woman she is today. MOM, you make me so proud, and I commend you for kicking your disease in the butt and becoming a better mother and overall, a better person. My world is better with you in it!!!!!

I am the youngest daughter of Chaplain Tammie. To start I want to say I am proud of the person my mother has become. Growing up with a mother who was an addict often left me feeling unwanted and unloved. These feelings led me searching for love in all the wrong places. I became co-dependent on others hoping to declare my own happiness. As a young adult I lacked self-esteem which caused me to think negatively of myself. Now that I am a mother of two daughters, I am now choosing not to blame my mom anymore and take control of my own life. I am now working with a therapist on correcting my own personal issues and trying to understand how addiction affects the whole family. I always thought growing up that if my mom really cared for us, we should be enough for her to stop. Now that I am older and know how addiction can truly blind a person of their priorities, I get it. I commend my mother for defeating every battle she faced because if I went through what she did I don't think I could win that fight. I forgave my mom a long time ago and am inspired by the woman she has formed to be. Mom, all I really want from this day forward is for you to love me and to build a healthy mom and daughter relationship. We cannot change the past, but we can look forward to what the future can bring.

Introduction

*S*omewhere around 1999, I swallowed a bottle of valium and was admitted to a psych ward for attempting suicide. During my first meeting with the psychiatrist, he wanted to know about my history. I shared with him my past sexual abuse and the many years I wasted in active addiction. I was full of tears as I spoke: he said to me, "drugs are not your problem; he said, "your problems are a heart matter." When I asked what he meant by that, he replied, "you are still living as a victim, you must deal with your heart matter by forgiving those involved and letting it go." He then said, "you cannot deal with your heart until you stop using drugs that you use to numb your hurt." He then said, "your loss of innocence has made you a victim of your circumstances. Only you can choose to continue being a victim or a victor"! Today I walk in the victory of my past with a heart full of forgiveness. Today I can share my history without shame but with a mindset to empower others so that they too can walk in freedom. God has given me the vision to share details of my past in this memoir platform. Because of years of drug use, dates and times may not be accurate, but the accounts are my truth. This memoir is about my struggles and victories, so I have chosen to respect the privacy of others. Before you start reading, I ask you please do not feel pity for me or be angry at me. Instead, praise God with me for His enduring love and redeeming quality. There is freedom through Christ Jesus. So, get comfortable, grab a tissue, and be encouraged as you go on this overcoming journey with me.

CHAPTER 1

Innocence Lost

I grew up in Seattle, Washington, mostly in low-income housing. I am what society calls bi-racial, my mother was white, and my father was Black. I have one brother with whom I grew up, four years younger. I do not remember many details of my childhood before the age of eleven, but I can recall bits and pieces. Not sure if the memory issues are because of all the years of drug use or because I am almost sixty, and my memory has lost its elasticity. I remember my mother taking us on picnics and other outings with her Caucasian single mom friends, who also had kids by Black men who seemed to have forgotten they were fathers. The first memory I have of my father was around eight years old. I remember he would come about in his nice white cars, sit around the table and drink alcohol with my mom and her friends. After that, I do not remember much more about him until I was fourteen. During this time is when I met my older siblings, whom my father's first wife conceived.

Around the age of ten, we moved out of Holly Park projects into a section eight house on Chasity Blvd. It was my mom, my brother and me. Shortly after moving, my mom brought this man home; his name was Chuck. Chuck did not fully move in, meaning he still had his own apartment but stayed with us a great deal of the time. Chuck being in our lives was the end of my childhood and the beginning of circumstances that I was too young to understand.

When Chuck first became part of our lives, he was kind to my mother, brother, and me. He bought my brother and me things my mother could not afford on her own. Since we were vulnerable kids who grew up without a father present, we grew to really like him, and it felt like we had a father. Chuck was lowering our defenses by inviting closeness, intimacy, trust, and reward. I cannot really give you accurate timelines or details, but I am about to share specifics of how a house of love turned to violence, abuse, loss of innocence, and trust.

During this period, my mom began drinking and partying every weekend with Chuck and his friends, who made our peaceful home into a weekend party house. In the beginning, it was fun for us kids as well. The adults would drink, play cards, dominoes, cook, and play loud music. It was a fun time for us, too, because Chuck would get silly and make us laugh with his drunkard humor. My mom would love to dance, so when they would get intoxicated, the slow jams would come on, and my brother and

I would watch the slow dancing begin. Now that I am an adult, I realize their behaviors were inappropriate for kids to witness. They were bumping and grinding while we watched.

Drinking on the weekends was the norm, but something changed quickly. Chuck began becoming more friendly toward me when intoxicated. He would have me sit on his lap to watch the adults play cards. I remember my mom would sit my brother on her lap; it seemed normal and fun for us kids to be included in the festivity. Not sure of the timeframe, but weekend fun shifted to weekend drinking ending in violence. Chuck and my mother would drink to intoxication and end with physical altercations.

During this time is when the abuse began. I cannot give a lot of details because professionals have told me that I mentally removed myself from the situation – a process psychologists refer to as 'dissociation' "This is because memories of traumatic events are laid down differently from everyday memories. Usually, we encode what we see, hear, smell, taste, and sense physically, as well as how that all slots together and what it means to us – and together, those distinct types of information together enable us to recall events as a coherent story. ("Education & Action Steps–OTC Title IX") But during traumatic events, our bodies are flooded with stress hormones. These encourage the brain to focus on the here and now, at the expense of the bigger picture." ("Why sexual assault survivors forget details–BBC Future") Because of this, I will not be able to give accurate dates, times, or real feelings, but what I will share with you is the truth of my abuse and destructive behaviors.

My most explicit memory is when I was eleven years old. My mom was cooking breakfast; Chuck was in the living room lying on the couch under a blanket, watching television. He called me over and asked me to lay by him, so I did. He began touching my vagina while my mom walked back and forth conversing with him. Chuck was grooming us all, "Grooming induces the transfer of shame from perpetrator to victim. This is no accident. For the abuser to continue to abuse, they need ongoing access to the victim for their crimes not to be uncovered. The abuser, therefore, grooms both the child and the family." Just writing this makes me feel sick to my stomach, asking myself why I did not tell mom or why she did know her daughter was in a crisis.

The partying, fighting, and drinking continued, and so did the abuse. I remember my mom passing out drunk, which was Chuck's quest to come to my room and fondle me. I remember he began rubbing his hard on me but not inside of me yet. I do remember feeling fearful, but I never told. I guess it was because of my mom's beatings, which left her black eyes on occasion. I do remember asking my brother to sleep with me at night to keep him from coming after me. Although I knew what he was doing to me was a secret, I have never told my brother that he was my saving grace on so many occasions. Chuck became physically abusive towards my brother during that period. Now that I am writing this, I understand now that Chuck was angry at my brother for interfering with Chuck's ability to fulfill his sick fantasies that only an experienced pedophile would have.

By the age of fourteen, Chuck was raping me. Because of my "dissociation," I cannot remember details of the trauma. "Children, especially, who feel helpless to do anything about the trauma, and disconnecting from the abuse or neglect (escaping, in a sense- dissociating) can allow them to cope." I thank God because I do not think I could continue writing if I did remember details. I remember that Chuck would look at me with this sick look during this period, and I hated it. My mom would allow him to walk around with just his underwear. I do remember him playing with his private and pulling it out when she would leave the room. I used to ask myself why she did not know that her perverted man was raping her daughter. It makes me sick and hurts my heart as I write this because I now understand why it is alcoholism. My mom was an alcoholic who turned a blind eye. She did not know her knight in shining armor was a seasoned child molester who was grooming her daughter.

Chapter 2

My Shameful Secret

When I started junior high school, guilt and shame began to surface; I did not know it at the time. In eighth grade, I remember gym class where we had to change our clothes in the locker room. I could not do it; I felt ashamed of my beautifully shaped body. The rapes were beginning to affect how I viewed myself, and I had low confidence and self-esteem. My mom and instructors thought I was just overly shy, but actually, I felt dirty and fearful that people would find out my secret if they saw my body; I felt scorned. "People who were sexually abused often see themselves as fundamentally bad even though they are not responsible for what happened. The shame of sexual abuse leads people to describe themselves as damaged or unworthy. They feel a sense of worthlessness and a desire to hide or disappear. Sadly, the self-esteem issues brought on by shame can create a cycle: a person's feelings of inferiority can lead to negative experiences reinforcing those feelings." ("Shame and Child Sexual Abuse Younique Foundation")

I was fifteen years old, just starting my sophomore year of high school, when I realized I missed my menstrual. I remember being so afraid and ashamed. How would I tell my mother her boyfriend has been having sex with me for years. During this time, I was allowed to have my first boyfriend; we would kiss and hold hands, nothing more. I was so desperate to produce a solution, so I decided to allow my boyfriend to go all the way. At the time, I was already six to eight weeks pregnant. He was a virgin and thought I was as well, so we so-called had sex. But really it was more like him trying to enter me and me pretending like it hurt. Because we all know a girl's first time is usually an uncomfortable experience.

My so-called plan worked, but I was still so fearful of telling my mom. Two months had passed, and I was now around sixteen weeks pregnant. Now that I am writing, I realize my mom had her suspicion. I remember getting out of the bathtub, drying off, and my mom busting in the bathroom. She looked at me and told me to come to talk to her when I was done in the bathroom. I remember being afraid of what would happen once I walked out of that bathroom. I finally got the courage to open that door and walk to my mom's room. She said you are not having an abortion or dropping out of school. She then asked was my boyfriend the father, and I said yes. I still feel a little shame and sadness to this day for telling that lie because he suffered for something he was innocent of. I am not going into any more detail about him except that I never pressured him for anything because I knew he was not the father.

Chuck was no longer living with us at the time but would come over on the weekends to party on occasions. The following weekend my mom told him I was pregnant. I remember Chuck looking at me and saying, "you are a slut." At this moment, I felt so dirty, although this man had taken my innocence from me, raped me for at least four years, and had the nerve to be angry because I had sex with someone other than him. What hurts me the most about this terrible violation is that He took away my choice as a woman, the choice of who and when I would give my virginity away, and I could never get it back.

Now that I am a mature adult walking in forgiveness and healing, I realize Chuck went for the weak and vulnerable, a common characteristic of child molesters or pedophiles. They see kids as objects to fulfill their sick fantasies, "sexual perversion in which children are the preferred sexual object." During therapy, I realized that he used seduction to gain my trust, which kept me silent. I feel nauseous and tearful while writing this, but I will not allow my emotions to have control. "Seduction is happening when the offender engages the victim in sexual activity by "seducing" them-courting them with attention, affection, and gifts. Just as one adult courts another, the pedophile seduces children over a period by gradually lowering their sexual inhibitions. Frequently his victims arrive at the point where they are willing to trade sex for the attention, affection, and other benefits they receive from the offender."

CHAPTER 3

The Walk Of Shame

*B*ack in the seventies, when high school girls were pregnant, they were labeled as easy or, as Chuck called me, "slut." Since I was considered a bad girl now that I was pregnant, I was transferred to an alternative school. I remember being so embarrassed by my pregnancy because of how my daughter was conceived and the lies I had to tell. I remember walking down my street from the school with my head hanging down to the ground. My next-door neighbor was looking out of her window, and I remember her saying, "hold your head up, do not be ashamed, do you not know babies are blessings from God." (As I write this four years later, I am tearful.) Her words made me feel like everything will be okay.

My daughter was born in April of 1978. I was in labor for over thirty hours, which was devastating because I was not yet sixteen. She was beautiful, and I did not associate her with him. Years later, I realized she looked like him since birth, but all I saw was a blessing. To this day, I still question if my mother really knew the truth all along. After giving birth, I chose to get my GED instead of continuing high school, which was a relief to me because I had low self-esteem and a heart full of secrets. For the next few years, I was not interested in having a boyfriend because of hidden issues from the abuse I had endured. To this day, I run into men that I went to school with, and they always compliment me on how I look the same and how all the guys had a crush on me back in the day. Boy, oh boy, this is just evidence that I had no self-confidence or self-esteem. I suppose I thought everyone saw me as dirty as I saw myself.

CHAPTER 4

Experiences With Love And Euphoria

*C*huck was no longer a part of our lives. He and my mother broke up for good. My daughter and I lived with my mother until I turned nineteen. My mother played more of the mother role, making most decisions because I was too young to manage, such a big responsibility. My mother did not want me to stop being a teenager, doing what teens do, like going to the movies and hanging over at a friend's house on the weekends. During that time, I only had one friend because back in those days, if you had a baby when you were young, you were considered being easy with the guys. Truth be told, I had never said yes to any guy I wanted to have sex with; I just happened to have a baby.

In 1981 when I was nineteen, my name came up on the housing list, and I was excited. My three-year-old daughter and I moved into our own place within walking distance of my mom's house. It was in Rainier Vista, part of the Seattle Housing Authority, which was known as the project. During this time, my only income was welfare and food stamps, so my mom taught me how to budget my finances. I was the first of my friends to have my own place, so it was a weekend hangout. We were not into hard drugs, but we did all smoke a little marijuana. I did not have a high tolerance, so it did not take much for me to get buzzed, act silly, and get the munchies. During this time, I met my first love. He was five years older than I was, and to my unknowing, he lived with his longtime girlfriend. Within six months, I was pregnant, and I was excited.

In August of 1982, I gave birth to another beautiful baby girl. The father was not involved much; he only called to come by at the most twice a week because he was committed to someone else. I finally wised up and made the decision the break it off with him when his live-in girlfriend came by my apartment banging on the windows in the middle of the night looking for him because his car was parked out front. Shortly after the breakup, I started hanging out with my neighbor across the street, smoking marijuana on occasions.

One night my neighbor called and asked if I wanted to get high. I said sure since the kids were in bed asleep. He walked in, asking me for a baby bottle, baking soda, and a cooking pot. He explained to me he had cocaine and needed those items to cook it into rock form called freebasing. When I hit the cocaine for the first time, I felt a powerful rush, feeling a warm rush through my body as soon as I inhaled it, it felt like an orgasm. However, I cannot say that I was instantly hooked; that came about a year later when the crack epidemic was rising. "In the early eighties, a cheap, highly addictive form of cocaine known as "crack" was first developed. Crack cocaine was popularized because of its affordability, immediate euphoric effect, and high profitability. The crack epidemic had particularly devastating effects within the African American communities of the inner cities by causing the increase of addictions, deaths, and drug-related crimes."

While the cocaine was cooking, there was a knock at the door; it was my baby's father with a friend of his. I remember hurrying to put away the drug utensils before opening the door. My daughter's father went to the bedroom where the baby was sleeping. All I can really remember him saying to me was, "I hope you get hooked." I was naïve when it came to drugs that I had no understanding of what it meant to be hooked. Honestly, looking back feels like he cursed me that night because, within a year, I was hooked.

During this time, neighborhood friends whom I smoked marijuana with began experimenting with marijuana laced with rock cocaine. We would all put in between four to five dollars to buy a bag of weed and a twenty-dollar piece of crack. We would pass the pipe around between four or five of us, have a good buzz, and call it a night. During this time, a neighbor lady who babysat for me informed me she had cocaine already rocked up for sale; the cost was twenty dollars. So, I bought one rock and went to search for the weed. I remember walking around the neighborhood with no luck finding weed, so I thought I would just smoke the rock without it. This was the beginning of twenty years of self-destruction. I was strung out on crack within a year, and my life had become unmanageable.

I was a mother of two daughters, working for the City of Seattle, making good money, but I never had money in my pocket. I would get paid every other Friday and barely had bus fair to last me to the next payday. I remember during this time; my mom noticed the change in me. I would drop my kids off to her to babysit and not pick them up until hours past the arranged time. She would buy diapers and make sure we had food to last until payday. One Saturday evening, my mom came over to my place and asked me what the cost was for one of those rocks I smoke, I told her the amount was twenty dollars. She handed me a twenty-dollar bill and told me to get one. I remember looking at her and saying why. She answered, "I want to see what it is about that drug that has changed you." I went across the street to get the rock cocaine. We sit at the kitchen table. When I returned minutes later, she hit the rock out of my weed pipe. I remember to this day the peaceful look she had on her face. She said, "now I see." No, she did not see because the first hit is the best; that pleasurable feeling is short-lived and leaves you willing to sell your soul to feel it again. Crack creates such an intense and euphoric high. Little did she or I know I would spend the next twenty years trying to recreate it. Crack slowly became an obsession that was beginning to dominate my life. One day a friend invited me to church. I said, "yes." I was not raised with any religion, so I had no idea what to expect, but what I received would be my strength through tough times to come. I remember sitting there, hearing the choir sing, and watching the people stand and say amen. Before I knew it, tears were rolling down my cheeks, and I was standing praising a God I knew nothing about. I continued attending church three or four more times before being baptized. My life did not change then, but I had an encounter with God, and His grace was with me. For the next twenty years, I experienced what I call a living hell before I could even begin to see myself as God saw me.

During this time, my best friend's brother had just returned from serving four years in the Airforce and stopped by my house to see how my two daughters and I were doing. He was really boring during our school days, so I never gave him a thought. To my surprise, he grew up to be a nice-looking man, and he began to show me interest. We started dating, and eventually, he asked the big question, and I said yes because he was good to my two girls and me. He was also a religious man, so sexual intimacy was something we saved for the wedding night. He had no idea that I struggled with an addiction; in my mind, he was saving me from my destructive addiction.

So, we got married and then came the wedding night. It was that night that I realized I was not in love. Before marriage, I had never lived with a man, so I did not know the range of sexual problems, including decreased sexual desire I had because of my past abuse. This caused tension in our marriage from the very beginning because sex is part of marriage. I continued to sneak off and smoke crack periodically, adding extra strain and distrust to our relationship.

Through the dysfunction, drug use, and attending church, time passed with no real change in my life. Except now I had two more beautiful daughters and an addiction that was a stronghold in my life. I still attempted to make something out of myself, hoping if I found something I was good at, it would take the place of the urge to self-destruct with drugs. I took a Certified Nursing Assistant course and began working at a Nursing home. I was assigned to the hospice unit, where young and old individuals were waiting to take their last breaths. At this time, I was not using drugs. I was a member of a church that my family would attend every Sunday. One day at work, one of my patients was taken off life support and was not expected to make it through the night. The following day when I got to work, the elderly lady was still alive. So, I had to go into her room and check on her periodically. While on the last rounds of my shift, I felt God urging me to pray for her. I hesitated because I had no idea how to pray. What I did was take her hand and talk to her.

I remember saying God wants her to repent with her heart and when you are done, squeeze my hand. Before I knew it, that lady squeezed my hand. I was speechless. I left the room and went to lunch. By the time I returned, she had died. I felt this joy in my heart because this was the first time God had used me for His glory.

A brief time after, all the joy I felt was gone. Crack once again took away my ability to care about anything but how I would get another hit. One morning I was headed to my dad's house after being up all-night doing drugs. I hoped he had left his key under the mat because I was too much of a mess to go home to my husband and four daughters. I remember getting in the elevator; a lady followed, and without thinking, I pushed her and grabbed her purse. I was arrested shortly after and taken downtown to the King County jail. I remember being so ashamed and afraid when the detective came in to talk to me. She knew I was not a criminal; I was twenty-six years old and had a clean record. She called my husband and told him they would release me to him if he could come down and show he had arranged treatment for me. My husband did just that. He took me and admitted me into Care Unit, which was substance abuse treatment in a hospital setting. During my twenty-one days stay, I was introduced to the twelve-step program.

Once discharged, I began going to church faithfully and felt forgiven and at peace. But I felt in my heart I had to ask the victim to forgive me. I knew her address because she lived in my dad's building. So, I wrote the letter that positively changed my life with negative consequences. The individual received the letter and felt afraid because I knew her address, she called the police, and robbery charges were filed against me that day.

During the crack epidemic of the 1980s, the justice system was absolutely flooded with new offenders. The legislation presented drug treatment as an option for first-time offenders. My attorney suggested that I put myself into a year-long drug treatment before I had to begin court proceedings. I did just that. I had spent five months at this inpatient facility in Edmonds, WA. My husband and kids would visit once a week, and I was getting physically and spiritually healthy. When it came time for my sentencing, the director of the treatment facility and my attorney were almost positive that I would get to do my time in treatment. The program director brought me to court on the day I was to go before the judge. I remember the judges, words clearly. He said, "I am tired of people coming to my courtroom using drugs as an excuse for their crimes. I sentence you to 31 months. You have two weeks to turn yourself in." At that moment, I realized I did not qualify for the drug court resolution because my offense was considered a violent crime, plus the victim is white, which was a strike against me as well. Once the shock was over, I realized I would have to leave my children and go into the unknown for twenty-one of those thirty-one months. But I tell you, what is meant for bad, God will turn it around for His good.

Going to prison ended up being the best thing that had happened to me since before my sexual abuse began when I was only eleven. My husband's aunt, a devout Christian visited me regularly. She sent me cassette tapes filled with worship music. My husband bought me a devotional Bible. I remember in prison; we had an hour a day to be outside. I spent the entire hour walking and worshipping God. During my time at Purdy the women's prison, I learned what it meant to have an intimate relationship with God. I learned to pray and talk to God; I learned that there is peace in every situation if I just keep my mind on Him. I learned that God talks to us through the Holy Bible. It was in prison that I learned that God would never leave me nor forsake me. Even though I was behind bars, I felt a sense of freedom that I had never felt before.

What I did not learn is that it is easier to be faithful to God when we are set apart from the world without the flesh being tempted. Today I know that true freedom and deliverance from our personal demons will not happen until we have the heart to forgive. I learned this the hard way once I was released back into society. Before I was released, I began experiencing seizures daily and was diagnosed with a seizure disorder that God would later heal.

CHAPTER 5

Home At Last

*I*n 1993, I was released and went back home to my children I no longer knew and a husband that stood by my side and cared for our children but was not equipped to care for a woman who had no idea how to love herself, let alone a man that unknowingly enabled her to continue to self-destruct. I remember a few days after being released, I went to the store and felt so lost. I went to the store knowing what I needed but felt instant anxiety while walking through that store. It seemed as if everyone was staring at me. I had spent the last two years isolated in prison. What I mean by isolated is that I kept to myself; I did not go there to meet friends. The entire two years I spent time with three individuals, they had been in prison a long time and were no longer into the drama that comes when you have a lot of traumatized, victimized, and violent women in closed quarters.

During the first two months home, we seemed like a happy family. We went to church on Sunday, where I continued to build a relationship with God. One Sunday, a lady stood before the church to testify how God had healed her of a seizure disorder. I remember sitting there listening to her story and believing in my heart that God was going to do for me, what He had done for her. When my husband and I got home, I got the medication I was prescribed for the seizures and dumped them in the toilet. My husband asked me what I was doing? My response was, what God did for that lady at church, he is going to do for me. From that day forward, I was healed and never had another seizure. Whenever I tell this testimony, I realize how God was with me through the journey we call life.

I decided to get back into the nursing field, so I registered to take a "Certified Nursing Assistant" refresher course so I could renew my license. Unfortunately, I was given the most devastating news after completing the course. Because of my criminal history, I could no longer work with vulnerable individuals. At that moment, I felt defeated because, once again, my past would continue to haunt me and stop me from moving forward. Even to this day, more than twenty years later, I still must explain my past during second interviews.

I have so much empathy for those individuals coming out of prison because the reality is people do not really see them. They see their rap sheets. I can testify to what former inmates face once released back into society. When released from prison, some psychological challenges can include discrimination, isolation, instability, and homelessness. "Because of systemic legal and societal barriers, once ex-offenders are released, it is more difficult for them compared to the general populace to find gainful employment, secure a consistent source of housing, and generally function in society. Often viewed as sub-citizens, ex-offenders are perpetually punished for crimes. The causes of these restrictions are systemic and affect ex-offenders at all levels of society." ("The Challenges of Prisoner Re-Entry into Society | Simmons") Later I will share how God sent me back to the prison system as an employee.

Within six months of getting the news that I could no longer have a career in nursing, I was right back on the pity pot-smoking crack. I rarely went to church, and when I did attend, I cried through the whole service while being tossed around the building while battling spiritual warfare. I was taught to believe that my life would be changed if I went to the altar on Sunday for prayer. But that did not happen for me because I had not absolutely surrendered my life to God, nor did I understand deliverance comes with continual sanctification. To spiritually surrender means to let go of control and trust God. "I have been crucified with Christ, and it is no longer I that live…" (Galatians 2:20).

Crack was the head of my life once again. Praise God for my mother, who stepped in countless times and took care of my kids for months at a time. I believe in my heart that she carried guilt for the trauma I suffered and taking care of my children was her way of making a sort of amends. (Today, I regret that I never took the time before she died to tell her that it was not her fault and that I love her. Likewise, my using drugs was not her fault. I was grown-up and responsible for the choices I made as an adult.) One fear I have today is that my children will have the same regrets regarding me when I pass on to glory.

My marriage was so dysfunctional. We lived apart more than together. For some reason, he kept coming back to save me. At that time in my destructive journey, I struggled to enjoy intimacy with my husband. Not because of anything he did wrong. It was because I was so wounded due to the extensive trauma I experienced as a young girl. It affected my emotional, psychological, physical, sexual, and spiritual well-being. Now I am aware that I was experiencing PTSD. Today I understand that it is almost impossible to love and enjoy sexual intimacy when a person is still enduring the pain of past sexual violation daily.

As for my kids, I really had no inclination of how I hurt and disappointed them until years later when they became teenagers. I know someone is reading this thinking how selfish, and you are right. I was so lost that I could not feel beyond my own pain that was stored in my soul. I was so deeply wounded and disintegrated that it felt like I had a thick protective wall around my heart that stopped me from receiving or giving love. As I am writing this memoir, I am experiencing feelings of sadness because I was so lost in addiction and pain from past trauma that, to this day, I cannot remember things a mother should. For example, I do not remember my baby's first step, the first day of kindergarten, graduation from sixth grade, and my oldest daughter's high school graduation. But praise God that I have forgiven myself just as Jesus Christ has forgiven me. My prayer for them is that they will wholeheartedly forgive me one day.

At the end of my marriage, my husband got so tired of worrying about me when I would run off to use drugs that he said, "you smoke your crack at home if the kids go to your moms for the night." So, Friday came, and we took my daughters to my mom's, and then we made the trip to Seattle from Kent to pick up the drugs. I felt relieved that I did not have to hide or walk the streets finding somewhere to smoke my crack. We got to the drug house, and my husband wanted to come to the dealer's house with me to be the police officer. I had to explain that is not how it works; it is against the street law to bring a stranger to a drug dealer's house. So, we got the drugs and went back to Kent, where the plan was, I would smoke the crack in our bedroom. I remember putting the crack and pipe on my dresser before I heard a knock on the door. It was a Jehovah's witness team. They kept me at the door, sharing their beliefs for about fifteen minutes. When I finally could make it back upstairs, I looked at my high husband. He had decided to try the crack, not just a small hit. He smoked the whole package in fifteen minutes. We traveled all the way back to Seattle to get more. By the end of the night, my husband said he would never smoke again and that he worked too hard to have it be gone in smoke in such a brief time, leaving you to only want more. I am so grateful for that because our kids needed at least one halfway sane parent. After that night, I returned to what I was used to, sneaking off when I got a chance to smoke in the streets or in strangers' homes.

Around 1995, my husband and I finally called it quits for good. Although we had this dysfunctional codependent relationship, we both knew that neither one of us was happy. "Codependence is a psychological condition or a relationship in which a person with low self-esteem and a powerful desire for has approval have an unhealthy attachment to another person. ("Signs of Codependency–What Addict & Codependent in ...") They place the needs of the other person before their own. A codependent person tries to satisfy the needs of another, who is often controlling or manipulative and who may have an addictive or emotionally unstable personality. Codependency is about damaged self-esteem, damaged functional boundaries, and an intense focus on pleasing other people while denying one's own needs and wants." ("Signs of Codependency–What Addict & Codependent in ...")

Throughout the years, I needed him to take care of me as much as he needed to take care of me. His taking care of me gave him a sense of purpose. Today I know how unhealthy codependency is for both parties involved.

What I have learned since that time is that people with codependency often form or maintain relationships that are one-sided, emotionally destructive, and/or abusive." Grateful today that we are both healthy and maintain a healthy relationship with each other for the sake of our daughters and grandkids. We spent ten years together, and I believe with all my heart that God placed him in my life for that season to help me to maintain some form of sanity and normalcy.

After our divorce, I was still a hot mess, smoking crack and maintaining my reputation as being a half-ass mom. Our kids initially remained with me, and we would be okay for short periods of time. When I did have an urge to use it, I had to find an excuse to leave the house. This caused more severe repercussions. For example, I would leave home for at least twenty-four hours without contacting my family. During the time I was away from home, I would put myself in dangerous situations. I would go to bad neighborhoods where they were known for having crack houses. I would be driving under the influence; lend my car to people I did not know.

This one time, I was at this drug house, and this guy said I could smoke in his place next door. Once we were there, I smoked up mine, and he shared his drugs with me. After the drugs were gone, he expected me to have sex with him as payback. I remember being terrified and saying no and headed for the door. That man came behind me and punched me in the back of my head. I remember feeling the pressure and grabbing the back of my head. My hand was full of blood, and the man panicked and dropped me off at Valley Hospital in Renton, WA. I had a mild concussion and five stitches.

Before entering the hospital, I tossed my purse in the garbage. I was preparing my story for the hospital staff about my injury. I told the ER I was mugged from behind, while walking down the street. It worked; they stitched me up and sent me on my way. The man's quick response to help me showed me he had lost perspective and reacted when he hit me, just like when I grabbed that lady's purse and ended up in prison.

I remember my mom saying, "when you are good, you are good, but when you are bad, you are bad." During my periods of abstinence, I was a patient and present mom. My girls were always clean, the house immaculate, and dinner was on the table by five; most importantly, I would be there when they needed me. When I was bad, drugs came first. Drugs made me selfish, and it was all about me. I would become emotionally unavailable trying to maintain my relationship with the crack that became the head of my life even though it made me crazy. Crack took precedence, and I gave it priority over my relationship with my family, which loved me and were so worried about my destructive behaviors.

I was never a social user. I was what you would call a binger, meaning, once I started, I could not stop until I had no more options for getting drugs. I remember times

I would tell my kids that I was going to the store and be gone for two days. For only a brief period of that time, I was using drugs, the other half of the time, I was getting up the courage to go back home to face my kids after lying to them once again. The excuse I would so often use to stay gone was, "I do not want my kids to see me high." The sad thing is I so-called did not want to disrespect my kids, but I sure would sit at another mother's house who did not mind me disrespecting hers and smoke crack. I remember the faces of someone else's kids when they would have to stay in their room while the other part of the house was used for smoking crack. When I got the courage to walk in the door, the kids would not be there. They would either be at my mom's, or their dad would have received a call from my mom, letting him know that I was gone, and the kids needed to be picked up. I would feel so relieved that I did not have to face the kids because of the guilt and shame I would feel. "I would only be thinking of myself." I would shower and fix myself up, attempting to look as normal as possible for the kids when they came home.

CHAPTER 6

Attempting At Love

*I*t was the year 1995 when my oldest daughter decided to set up a blind date with a friend's father who coached at the high school she was attending. I can remember opening my front door and feeling instantly attracted. We went out to dinner, drinks, and live music. We were connected from that moment on for close to a year. Shortly after we started dating, I had to move from my apartment due to owing back rent. He came to the rescue and invited my four daughters and me to come and live with him. We moved into his small apartment for about a month before moving to a bigger apartment. Everything started out so wonderful. Since I had been abstinent from drugs for a few months, I was able to get a job as the main cook at a friend's restaurant. My relationship was going well. We were on our way to falling in love. The best part of the relationship was the intimacy and passion we felt for each other. In this relationship, I realized that I could enjoy sexual pleasure without worrying about my past. We both mutually felt that this relationship was going places. But I had a secret that I had not revealed: my drug addiction.

While working at the restaurant, I met the owner's sister; she worked as the cashier for a few hours a week. She had two daughters the same age as my youngest daughters. During this time, she would invite me to Church, but I would find a reason not to go because I was living with a man and not married. Today I know we do not have to come to God perfect and fake because he knows everything we have done. He just wants us to come and allow him to perfect us. "Come to me, all you who are weary and burdened, and I will give you rest. Take my yoke upon you and learn from me, for I am gentle and humble in heart, and you will find rest for your souls. The scripture says, "For my yoke is easy, and my burden is light."

The first few months of this relationship went great; I stayed clean and enjoyed the love I was shown. He and I had this physical attraction full of passion and genuine respect. During this relationship, I realized I could enjoy sexual intimacy with a man if my heart were in it. A few months after we started living together, I cut my hand severely at work which needed surgery to repair the damage to my nerves and tendons. I was off work for two weeks and started visiting with a neighbor who was an alcoholic. One day her brother stopped by her house to tell his sister he had some for sale. Before he left, I bought a twenty-dollar rock. I would sneak to her house for the next two months to get high. My man at the time had no idea what I was going through because I was maintaining going to work and taking care of the household.

One day I was cleaning and came across my boyfriend's checkbook. Without hesitation, I wrote a check to an individual who sold me some crack. A month goes by before he gets his bank statements and notices the forged check. He did not know yet that I had written the check. After a few days of him trying to figure out who had done this, I confessed. I remember he cried; he was so hurt that I would steal from him. I cannot remember what reason I gave him for writing the check, but I do remember our relationship was over. He contacted his bank and told them that I had written the check. The following day I had to go to the bank and sign an agreement to pay it back, or forgery charges would be filed. The trust was broken and could not be restored. My boyfriend took his name off the lease and moved out the following month. My addiction spiraled out of control once again, and eventually, I was evicted from that apartment.

CHAPTER 7

My First Psychosis

F all of 1996, I was living in a two-bedroom apartment with my three youngest daughters. I had been abstinent for a few months and was still working at my friend's restaurant. My oldest daughter had graduated high school that same year and was living with a roommate. Next door lived a young man and his girlfriend; they were in their early twenties. I remember hearing a lot of traffic coming from their apartment. What I mean by traffic is people coming and going throughout the night. I knew they were selling drugs. So, one evening after work, I knocked on the door and asked them if they knew where I could buy some crack. He was hesitant initially, but eventually, he let me in and sold me forty dollars' worth of crack.

This was the first time I had the drug at my doorstep in ten-plus years of smoking crack. Daily I would leave work with thirty to forty dollars in tips. Before going home, I would stop by my neighbor's apartment to spend most of my tips on drugs. Once home, I would hurry to cook and get the three girls to bed so I could smoke. This went on for maybe two weeks before. Now it is Friday the first of the month, and the rent is due. I remember hurrying home to attempt to pay my rent before the office closed, but I did not make it in time. I told myself that I could get a small amount of crack and put the rest of the rent money away until Monday morning, when the office opened.

Kids were in bed, and I smoked crack all night. I am unsure how often I went next door for another thirty-dollar rock. I remember beginning to feel paranoid. I felt like something, or someone was moving around my apartment. I would go to the kids' room to check, and they were all sleeping. I finally told myself that I was just tripping from smoking too many cracks in a short amount of time. So, I decided it was time to finish the last of the crack and take a shower. I remember getting my shower water ready. I then packed the rest of the crack on my pipe. I hit it and held it in; I exhaled once I got into the shower.

Instantly I began experiencing delusion but did not realize it at the time. In my mind, I heard someone twisting the bathroom doorknob. They were saying open the door and come out; I responded by saying okay, I will be out in a second. I continued to hear people talking in my bedroom. I also heard voices instructing my kids to go back to their rooms. In my delusional state, I thought the police must be here, and they must have been watching me go next door all night. Finally, when I opened the door,

I saw no one. I walked to the living room, where I instantly felt a cold breeze. I thought the police had taken my kids out of the patio door and left it open. I went to the patio door, and it was shut and locked. Now I am so confused. I went to my kids' room, and they were all sleeping in their beds. At that moment, I realized I must be having a mental breakdown because no one was there, and no one was coming. I remember crying to myself, feeling so confused and afraid of what had just happened to me. I finally called the one person I knew who would help me without judgment. I called my ex-husband's aunt, who stood by me when I was in prison.

I explained to her the best I could through the tears I had experienced. She asked if I wanted to go somewhere for help, and I quickly answered yes. She called me back in a few hours; she had planned for me to go to a faith-based program for addicts the following morning. That night my mom and my brother came to my place to pick up my kids. I remember they were mad because I was asking for help and leaving them to clean up my mess. They stored some of my furniture and kept my kids for about three months. When I look back, a cool breeze was the presence of God taking control of the atmosphere because the storm I was in was too big for me to manage. I spent two months at Victory Outreach where I focused on building my relationship with God and learning bits and pieces about spiritual warfare and how my drug use was a door opening for the devil to control my mind in hopes of destroying my purpose. "It would be another ten years of active drug use before I learned how to shut that door on the mind-binding stronghold that has stolen my self-worth."

After leaving Victory Outreach, I stayed with my dad for two months while waiting for my settlement from labor and industries for the injury I sustained at the restaurant. The check was for five thousand dollars. This was enough for me to get an apartment for my daughters and myself. Since I had two evictions, my dad co-signed an apartment in Kent, WA, for me. I had been clean for four months and was working through temporary employment agencies.

During this time, my mother and I thought it was time for me to tell my daughter the truth about who her father was. I cannot remember the details of what transpired when she was told the truth. But I do know she wanted to meet him, and my mother volunteered to arrange the meeting. From what I was told, my mother and daughter showed up at his house, and once he saw my daughter, he called for his sons to come downstairs and meet their sister. In the beginning, I would ask my daughter about the visits, but I had to stop because I would get these strong feelings of sadness which I now know as a spirit of depression creeping into my soul. I am unsure how my mother felt sitting talking with the man she once was intimate with who sexually violated her daughter while she was under the same roof. I can imagine her having many nights of tears filled with shame and remorse. My daughter was able to spend nine years getting to know her father before he passed away in 2008. My natural self does not understand why she would want to know him. However, my parental side does understand that my daughter grew up without understanding what unconditional love from a parent looked like. So why not get to know the other parent who could possibly fill the voids that were missing in her life.

CHAPTER 8

Starting Over Once Again

$\mathcal{M}$y dad and I signed the lease, I began moving my belongings, and I met my first neighbor. She came out and introduced herself and asked if I needed any help. She then said if you need anything, come by, and ask, and I kept that back in my mind for a later date. Later that week, my three daughters moved back home, and everything went well for a few months. I reconnected with my friend from the restaurant who lived not far from me. She would pick my two youngest daughters and me up every Sunday for church. She was married and had grown up in the Pentecostal Church; she became somewhat of a mentor to me for a season of my journey. During this same time, I found out my fifteen-year-old daughter was pregnant. After the initial shock wore off, we were excited. I could not be mad at her when I was the one who failed as a parent. She was only fifteen and I would give her permission to hang out later than I should have because I wanted to smoke crack without having to hide or answer my teenage daughter when she began questioning my erratic behavior.

I also started dating a man I had met years ago when I worked for the housing authority. He was handsome, caring, and kind. He knew that I had struggled with addiction. He smoked crack from time to time but had better control over it than I did. I worked in Bellevue then and did not have a car, so my current man would pick me up from work each day and drop me off at home. I remember it was Thanksgiving eve. He had picked me up from work. During the ride home, we talked about what we would have for Thanksgiving dinner. This year my mother, brother, and his family came to my house for dinner. This would be the first-time dinner would be at my house in years. We were driving and came to light in Renton, and my man says I want to get high. When he first said that I was not triggered or interested because I had not used it in about six months, and things were going well for me. I remember us being at a light when he said I wanted to get high again. I responded this time with, "are you sure?" He said, "yes." I said, "make a turn here," and directed him to a drug dealer I knew in the neighborhood. See, this man and I had never used drugs together, so he did not know that once I got started, I did not know how to stop.

We smoked crack most of the night. When morning came, we went back to my apartment to prepare dinner for my family, that would be arriving around three o'clock. I got home put the turkey in the oven, called someone to bring me more drugs, and attempted to finish this meal. The closer it got to three, the more anxiety I felt. Finally, I had to get out of there. I could not face my family high; I could not let them see me and feel their disappointment again, so I left before they arrived. I caught a cab to a dealer's house and ended up in a motel room. I called my man-friend at about eleven pm, and he came and picked me up and took me home. My kids left with my family, and I felt like crap again. He was very tearful and apologetic, stating I did not know. Most Americans use drugs at least once in their lifetime or even socially without becoming addicted. But those with pre-existing emotional vulnerabilities (trauma, anxiety, mental health disorder, PTSD) will more than likely become addicted.

I remember starting 1999 off on a three-day binge with my neighbors that seemed to last for eleven long months. I was on a rollercoaster ride and did not know how to get off. At this point, I realized once again that my life had become unmanageable, but I continued to stay high. My daughter had her beautiful baby boy, whom I loved. One day after binging over the weekend, I was desperate for more drugs. I remembered that my grandson had bags of brand-new diapers in the closet. I returned the diapers to the store and bought drugs. My daughter was so hurt and disgusted with me that she called my mom and moved out. You would think this would have been my bottom nut. But, no, it was not. I continued to stay high. My father was on my lease, so he paid my rent when I neglected to do so myself. People may think he enabled me to continue my use, but that was not the case. He was protecting his credit and vowed never to cosign again.

I remember getting high for a few days with my neighbors during this time. It was a Sunday morning, and we were all high, and I said to them that I was going to church up the street for their night service that started at six pm. I left the neighbor's house at about five o'clock to shower and get ready for church. I stopped by the neighbor's house on my way to church and asked for one more hit. They laughed and gave me the hit, and I blew it out and made my way to church. I stayed for prayer and felt the presence of God. I walked back home and did not stop by the neighbor's house. For the next two months, I stayed away from where the drugs were and focused on reading my Bible and hanging out with my friend, which was a positive role model. She had no idea of my struggles with addiction. During this time, I spent more time reading my bible, and to my surprise, I began getting a hunger to read more. God was imparting His word into my heart because He knew the devil was not done with his attempts to destroy me. It was imperative that I began to know God's promises so I could fight in the spirit to keep my sanity through the dark times that would keep me feeling hopeless and lost. Things were good for a short while until the devil came knocking again, but this time, he was trying to kill me physically because I was already spiritually dead.

CHAPTER 9

My First Suicide Attempt

I had a tough time dealing with the reality that the man who took away my innocence was now an important part of my daughter's life. Depression and feelings of hopelessness had become a more significant factor in my life, along with continued drug use. I had spent years keeping my abuse buried under my drug addiction, and when it came back to the surface, I did not know how to cope. My innocence was stolen beginning at the age of eleven. I am now thirty-six years old and had never gone to any therapy. I had a long history of drug treatment that only focused on my drug use, not the reasons that led me to self-medicate with drugs. So now, I am this eleven-year-old little girl living in the body of this dysfunctional thirty-six-year-old drug addict whose life and well-being are compromised, and I have lost my will to live.

I remember driving down the highway and this song was playing, and a verse in the song was "nothing else matters." It was a cassette tape, so I kept rewinding it repeatedly to that one verse "nothing else matters." To me, this meant nothing in this life mattered. I went to this bar and saw an old friend of a friend. What I meant by old is old in age. I knew he had cancer and other health issues, which meant he most likely had pain pills or something I could use to end my life. I was in Seattle on Rainier in one of those old neighborhood bars. I told him that I was too drunk to drive back to Kent. He offered to let me stay the night at his house. The first thing that I did was to look in his medicine cabinet. I was right; he had a bottle full of valium. He said I could use his room for the night while he slept on the couch. I opened the whole bottle of pills and swallowed them all. Instantly this cool feeling goes through my body. I went to the room, curled in a ball, and asked God to forgive me because suicide was a sin.

I had heard people say in church that those who commit suicide go to hell because they do not have time to repent. So, I took a chance and repented for what I was about to do. After telling God I was so sorry for what I was doing, I lay there with tears rolling down my face hoping I would make it to heaven. "For those who have never experienced suicidal thoughts, it can sometimes be difficult to understand why someone would choose to die by suicide. However, those who attempt suicide or who die by suicide is not doing so because they do not care about the people in their life. Often, they are in so much pain that they feel it is their only choice, and that it would be better for everyone that way." (spunout).

The next thing I heard was someone calling my name, "I thought it was God calling me." After that, I kept hearing a male voice saying, "Tammie, breathe. You haven't been breathing for five minutes." I then remember opening my eyes to a room full of paramedics. They had used Narcan to get my heart pumping again. I was later told that the man whose house I was at heard me grunting loudly, like gasping for air, which led him to call 911.

I was transported to the hospital and later transferred to Detox where I received a prophetic word. I arrived at the detox late in the evening; I was not sure what I was feeling. The gentlemen who did my intake came into the office with a tub of water and began taking off my shoes. I asked him what he was doing? He stated, "Jesus washed all his disciple's feet." I cried uncontrollably because I knew it was from God. When Jesus washed the disciples' feet, He told them (and us), "I have given you an example, that you should do as I have done to you" (John 13:15). As His followers, we are to emulate Him, serving one another in lowliness of heart and mind, seeking to build one another up in humility and love." Although this man did not know me or my religious views, he was acting in love. It felt like God was saying to me you are my disciple, and I know the plans I have for you. This experience was a miracle from God that I could not yet understand or receive whole-heartedly. God was attempting to open my eyes so I could see the plans He had for me. I was like a newborn baby; I could see a glimpse of light and shadow figures but could not see Him clearly.

The following day, I was talking to another staff member who was very rude to me. I remember crying and telling the man I was supposed to be dead. He instantly changed being rude to me to being concerned. He asked me if I wanted to go to the hospital for a little while I said yes. He called my mother and informed her I was being transferred to St Francis hospital on suicide watch. During my first meeting with the psychiatrist, he wanted to know about my history. I shared with him my past sexual abuse and my years of addiction. I was full of tears. He then said to me, "drugs are not your problem." He said, "your problems are a heart matter." When I asked what he meant by that, he replied, "you are still living as a victim, you must deal with your hurt forgive, and let go." He then followed, "you cannot deal with your heart until you stop using drugs to hide your hurt."

That same day I called my mother in tears and told her that I could not manage life and was not in a good place to take care of my two younger daughters who were still in my care. This was the first time in years that I felt my mother's genuine empathy for me. So, she took care of my two daughters for six months while I got my head together.

I gave up my apartment and all my belongings except for my clothing and moved near downtown Seattle to a brand-new woman's transitional program. To be in the program, you had to be in outpatient treatment for addiction or mental health. I was court-ordered to complete outpatient substance abuse treatment which I did while in the program. During this time, I worked as a housekeeper through the millionaire's club and took a certificate course in office management. Things were going well; I was clean, sober, and attending church every Sunday. During this time, I told my testimony for the first time in front of strangers. I attended a Church of God in Christ called Tolliver Temple in Seattle. The Church of God in Christ is a trinitarian Holiness-Pentecostal denomination. The church teaches three separate and distinct works of grace that God performs in the life of believers: salvation, entire sanctification, and the baptism or infilling of the Holy Ghost."

I would catch the bus to church on Sundays and sit in the back of the church. At that time, the women in the sanctified churches did not wear pants and wore big hats. The only time a woman would preach would be the fifth Sunday of the month which ends up being three or four times a year. I remember church lasting about three hours. The first hour would be the choir singing beautiful and heartfelt gospel songs; they would bring me to tears. Following would be a praise break where the drums and organ would play loudly, and people will be dancing and praying in the spirit. I remember many times I would be in the back of the church pacing back and forth and praying in the spirit. Other times I would be in the back of the church being tossed around by the devil. I was in the middle of spiritual warfare battling mind-binding strongholds of being unforgiving and addiction. While I was attending the Pentecostal church, I looked sanctified all dressed up but on the inside. Still, I was fighting a war. 2 Corinthians 10:3-4 says, "For though we walk in the flesh, we do not war after the flesh: (For the weapons of our warfare are not carnal, but mighty through God to the pulling down of strong holds;)." A stronghold of the mind is a lie that Satan has established in our thinking that we count as true but is a false belief. When we embrace these lies, they affect our attitudes, emotions, and behaviors.

Every fifth Sunday was organized by the women's department of the church; the speaker for that service was usually an Evangelist, Missionary, or the Pastors wife. The Sunday before the fifth Sunday, the Pastor's wife came to me and asked me if I would share my testimony the next week. I quickly said yes without giving it a thought. After I said yes, I wanted to run to her and say no, I could not because I had secrets that I was too ashamed to share. I was a drug addict who had been sexually abused as a kid; I am tainted. I have kids who do not live with me because I am too much of a mess to care for them. But I did not say a word and spent the week writing my testimony. Sunday morning came, and I thought I was ready until I got to the church. I arrived a few minutes late and saw all these sanctified people who focused on living holy and looking the part. I remember when the Pastor's wife introduced me, I walked up to that podium shaking like a leaf. I shared not in detail but the outer surfaces of my life. Once I began speaking, I felt empowered by God's presence. I was tearful as I shared my truth.

When I said I did not know that Jesus loved me at the time of my suicide attempt, my testimony moved the church audience. They yelled, "amen, sister, give God all the praise." Once I finished and was walking from the podium, the Evangelist from California grabbed my hand and prophesied into my life. She stated. "God is going to use you in a mighty way through your testimony, but the devil is going to try and kill you first." At the time, I had no idea what she meant by the devil is going to try and kill me. I ignored that part and focused on the excitement I felt about God wanting to use me. This experience is an example of how God can use us in the middle of our mess. Reminds of the phrase, "God is not done with me yet."

The next week I was walking in downtown Seattle, and I walked by an unhoused individual lying in the doorway of a department store. He asked me whether I had any change; my response was no; I do not have change. As I walked away, I heard the spirit of God say, "yes, you do have change." I remember feeling so convicted that I walked back and handed that individual all the change I had in my pocket. That was the start of God transforming my heart to resemble His heart. "Mathew 25:44-45 reads; Then they will reply, 'Lord, when did we see you hungry or thirsty or a stranger, naked, or sick or in prison and did not do anything to help you?' Then he will answer, 'I assure you that when you haven't done it for one of the least of these, you haven't done it for me.'" This verse is a reminder that God is everywhere. Sometimes it can be hard to sense His presence in environments we're not used to or when we encounter a stranger in need.

A brief time after sharing my testimony at the church, I completed treatment and an office administration course. I had six months clean off crack and was employed at Bellevue Cadillac as a receptionist. I was now living in Kent in my own apartment with my two youngest daughters. Things were going well until I met some neighbors who smoked crack. Not long after meeting them, I began going by their place on weekends to purchase crack for myself. Eventually, I lost my employment at the car dealership and started working for temporary agencies. Most people ask what happened? God just used you at church, and now you are going backward. Back then, I did not understand myself, but today I know it was a flesh matter.

I was saved, meaning I believed in Jesus as the son of God who died so I could be free, but I was not yet delivered from my personal demons. Meaning I had encounters with God but had not surrendered my will, which was a soul matter. When Jesus died and was buried, the filthiness of our flesh life was thrown into the grave, stripped of its power (Romans 6:3-7). When He rose again, we in our new creation rose with Him on high. Paul exhorts us to yield our body to serve Christ, not sin, for sin no longer has power over us (Romans 6:13-14). The answer is that I did not know the meaning of bondage or what it meant to walk out of my freedom. I still had sin in some areas of my life. Some people say you cannot be saved and still sin. I disagree. God meets us where we are. Meaning I was not raised in the church and had not come to believe in Jesus until I was in active addiction. Mark 16:17 "And these signs will accompany those who believe in my name they will cast out demons; they will speak in new tongues."

I realize now what was missing was knowledge and understanding of what it really meant to be born again and the power I had within to walk out of my deliverance. This did not happen until years later when I grabbed onto God's outstretched hand and was pulled out of the place of darkness. 2 Corinthians 5:17 Therefore if any man be in Christ, he is a new creature: old things are passed away: behold, all things are become new.' We are New Creations in Christ, but it was not so easy for me to live and walk in freedom because I didn't realize the truth of God's word. Meaning I did not fully understand what the suffering of Christ had done for me on Calvary.

I recently came across this song called "Deliver Me" by Donald Lawrence featuring Le'Andria Johnson. At the beginning of the song, Donald says, "Sometimes our souls have holes in them due to things that have happened in the past; hurt, abuse, molestation, divorce, but we want to speak to you today and tell you that God wants to heal the hole in your soul. Some people's actions are not because their spirit is wrong, but it is because the past has left a hole in their soul."

According to the dictionary, the soul is the union of body and spirit, which some prefer to call the mind. "Empty Soul" represents the lack of the very essence of life, a total void of wills, a finding of abandonment." This shows how my spirit was right for years because I had accepted Jesus, which meant his spirit dwelled within me. The problem was that I had never healed from my past, which made it a struggle for me to renew my mind. My mind was full of un-forgiveness and feelings of low self-worth instead of love which is the first thought in the mind of Christ.

CHAPTER 10

Consequences Of Lukewarm Christianity

*L*ike my mother told me years earlier, when I am good, I am good, but when I am bad, I am bad. I was either in the light attempting to know God, or I was in the dark giving into the flesh smoking crack. The Bible reads: "I know your deeds, that you are neither cold nor hot. I wish you were either one or the other! So, because you are lukewarm—neither hot nor cold—I am about to spit you out of my mouth" (Revelation 3:15-16). Being lukewarm in our faith is a red flag, signaling our hearts are not where they should be. In fact, God makes a strong statement about those who go down this path in the Old Testament book of Isaiah. "The Lord says: 'These people come near to me with their mouth and honor me with their lips, but their hearts are far from me. Their worship of me is based on merely human rules they have been taught "(Isaiah 29:13). See, I was attending church focusing on the religious aspects, which are the rules and regulations made by man. I was serving man, not God. My heart continued to be corrupted, unpredictable, and weak every time I was presented with a test. For the next two years, I grew my criminal record from being a one-time felon to a two-time felon, along with a few misdemeanors in between.

In 2001, I was charged with forgery as I attempted to cash a check on an account that belonged to my daughter. I was arrested on the spot, pleaded guilty, and was sentenced to treatment and community service. In 2002 I was also charged and pleaded guilty to theft. In addition, I took my daughter's car without her permission. I was sentenced to 24 months of probation. Eventually, I served forty days in jail for failure to pass a clean UA.

As I write my record information, I am tearful and grateful for Jesus. I cannot always have the final say. What we see as a mess, God sees as a bed of roses pruning for His glory. "The pain of spiritual pruning results from our reluctance to give up whatever inhibits our growth in God."

Serving forty days in jail was a blessing in disguise. I spent the time reading my Bible and attending worship services when they were offered. During this time, I could feel a renewing passion for God being birthed. Once I was released, I stayed off the crack and focused on getting employment through temporary services. Finally, I was stable enough to move to a different area with my two daughters. We lived in Auburn, Washington, close to my mother and one of my older daughters.

Not long after moving in, I recognized one of the neighbors who lived in the duplex across the street. He was a nice guy who, a few years earlier, had invited me to go sailing with him and his friends. The plan was for me to stay at his place while he worked the graveyard shift so we could meet up with his friends the following morning after he got off work. That evening he picked me up and dropped me at his place while he went to work. Once he left, I began smoking the crack I had brought. Eventually, all the crack was gone, and so was my money. So, I began snooping around his apartment and found fifty dollars. I took the money and bought more drugs with it. When morning came, it had started raining, so the sailing trip was canceled, and I was dropped off at home. The next day he called me and nicely asked did I take his money. I quickly denied it, but he knew different. I had not seen him since that time until I became his neighbor. I would do my best not to look his way. When he did see me, he avoided looking my way. I knew I needed to make amends, but I did not dare to face him, so I did not acknowledge him.

During this time, I started much-needed therapy. During one of my sessions, I was sharing about my childhood abuse and how I have had thoughts of suicide after the perpetrator became a part of my daughter's life. During this session, she informed me that I could bring a civil suit against him since I realized being a victim of childhood sexual abuse has impacted me my entire life negatively. I sent a letter to three different attorneys who take cases pro-bono. I received a call from an attorney, I met with her, and she said we have a case. She filed a civil suit. I explained to my daughter what I was doing and reassured her it had nothing to do with her; it was about what he did to me and how it has affected my mental health.

CHAPTER 11

I Found My Soulmate

Shortly after moving into my apartment, my neighbor next door came by saying she could hear my gospel music blaring out of my apartment. The following week she knocked on my door and asked me to attend church with her the next Sunday, and I agreed. She went on to say that we would be riding with a neighbor. When Sunday morning came, I went out to the car that was waiting to find a handsome man named Will as our chauffeur. We were introduced and proceeded on our journey to Tacoma, where the church was located. I was sitting in the back seat and noticed the handsome driver looking at me through his rear-view mirror. After church, I made my way back home. Again, I noticed Will watching me through the mirror. Once we were back home, he asked me if I would be interested in a ride to church the next Sunday. I said yes. The next Sunday, it was just him and I and it was an instant attraction. Since he lived just a few doors down, we would spend every evening together sitting on his deck smoking cigarettes and talking. He was a divorced father of two adult sons and had one grandson he adored. Like me, his addiction got in the way of him being the father and husband he desired to be. His drug of choice was crack cocaine; at the time of our meeting, he had four years clean and was rebuilding strong relationships with his sons.

Shortly after meeting my two daughters, Will and I attended church every Sunday. We were also engaged in premarital sex. In the beginning, we did not feel conviction about it. We would joke around about repenting to God; today, I know God was not pleased with our behavior.

One Sunday in Church, I got the revelation of what God's Word says about sex before marriage. Hebrews 13:4 considers sex outside of marriage to be immoral. "Let marriage be held in honor among all, and let the marriage bed be undefiled, for God will judge the sexually immoral and adulterous." After church, I told Will that I was feeling convicted by the message and that I was going home to pray and repent.

"Repentance isn't just an attitude of the heart; it literally means to turn from the former life with a commitment to change for the better." This was the first time during my years of trying to live for God the word of God brings such a strong conviction that I received and obeyed. "To be convicted is to experience an utter dreadfulness of sin. Our attitude toward sin becomes that of Joseph, who fled temptation, crying out, "How could I do this great evil and sin against God?" (Genesis 39:9). The Holy Spirit not only convicts' people of sin but also brings them to repentance (Acts 17:30). The Holy Spirit brings to light our relationship with God. The convicting power of the Holy Spirit opens our eyes to our sin and opens our hearts to receive His grace (Ephesians 2:8). (https://www. gotquestions.org/conviction-of-sin.html.)

The next week after church, I was getting out of Will's car, and I saw the gentleman across the street from whom I had stolen money a few years prior. Again, I felt conviction for not only stealing the money but lying about it after I was caught. So, I went across the street and knocked on his door. His live-in girlfriend answered the door, and I asked her if I could speak to them both outside. They came to the porch, and I confessed to stealing from him and lying to him. I was tearful; he hugged me and said I accept your apology. His girlfriend hugged me and said I have so much respect for you, and I know it took courage to come over here. After that day, we spoke and waved when we saw one another. I felt so relieved for following the leading of the spirit of God to do the right thing and make amends. I also learned that making amends freed me from guilt and anxiety it brought me closure to negative emotions that I brought on myself.

During this time, I was coming to the end of my civil suit against the predator that stole my innocence. We were preparing for a litigation hearing; I remember telling my attorney that it was not about the money; I wanted him to take responsibility and apologize for what he had done to me. I never did get an apology because he did not have the courage to admit he was wrong. I remember my daughter telling me that he talked about it as if we were in a relationship. This was an example of his sick distorted thinking to rationalize and justify his crime. During all the court hearings, he had his attorneys represent him in his absence due to medical issues. I remember being in court, going before the judge for him to decide if we had a case. The judge told his attorney to get a mediator and produce an offer because I had a clear case that deserved justice.

One month later, we had mediation; we were there for approximately four hours with the attorneys negotiating. I accepted a cash payment of fifty thousand dollars that was ordered to be paid within thirty days, and my daughter was added to his will along with his other three children.

CHAPTER 12

We Got Married

Before I received the settlement, Will and I were married by our Pastor. The ceremony was small; we just had two witnesses, the Pastor, and his Wife. We were in love, and the kids were adjusting to the change. During this time, he was working, and I was unemployed and receiving child support for my two younger daughters. During this time, I spent my days reading and studying the Word of God. Kids were doing good; for the most part, they were happy to have some stability in the house. They did not have to wonder whether I would be home after school or in the mornings when they woke. Will had two adult sons and a two-year-old grandson. While his sons were growing up, Will struggled with addiction, but their relationships were good because he had turned his life around in the past four years. Will also had a younger brother that lived here in Washington and other siblings, and his mother lived out of state, so I did not have the opportunity to meet them in person until a much later unpleasant time.

Finally, the big day arrived, and I received my settlement. After attorney fees and other costs, I cleared 29,000. When the money came, the thought of drugs did not cross my mind. The first thing I bought was a car and then the kids a computer. Next, I bought the kids new beds and a new living room set. My mom, who had worked hard all her life, complained about her back hurting. So, I bought her a new bed. When we went shopping for the bed, I remember she kept passing by the ones that looked the most comfortable because of the price. Finally, I told her to get the one she wanted, and she deserved something comfortable. My thoughts were it was the least I could do for her. Because for one, she was my mom; second, she had always been there for my kids when I could not be because of my addiction.

About a month after receiving the money, Will told me I should slow down with the spending. My response was that I suffered for years and will enjoy spending every dime of this money. By this time, I had about $12,000 left from my settlement, so I decided the following week I would take half of what was left and open an account at a credit union that I could not touch without a penalty. Monday morning arrived, Will went to work, the kids went to school, and I planned to go to the Boeing Credit Union to open the account. Before going to the credit union, I decided to stop in the Fred Meyer in Renton.

While waiting to check out, a lady I knew from two years ago was in front of me. We were catching up with each other's lives. She mentioned that she had just moved into a new place and invited me to come by for coffee. I followed her to her place, which was the worst choice I could have made. I forgot to mention this lady who was a professional medical assistant during the day and a crack smoker at night. I ended up staying at her house for a few hours, smoking crack. When I left her house that afternoon, the only thing on my mind was, "where can I get some more drugs." My routine for the past six months was to have dinner done by five when my new husband got home, but this day I had allowed the drugs to overpower my decision-making. The research described in this issue (see "New Avenues of Research Explore Addiction's Disrupted and Destructive Decision Making") shows that drug addiction is associated with altered cortical activity and decision making that appears to overvalue reward, undervalue risk, and fail to learn from repeated errors.

I started driving south, and I remembered that a girl I knew from my past lived in Auburn, maybe ten minutes from my house. I asked her to call somebody who could deliver crack when I arrived. She was happy to do it. She was one of those people that got high by allowing people to get high at her place. It is now about seven pm. I remember it was starting to get dark outside; by this time, I had turned off my cell phone because I knew that my husband or kids would be calling until I answered. While waiting for the dealer to show up at the girl's house, there was a knock at her front door, and it was Will, telling me to come outside. He could tell by looking at me that I was high. I remember him telling me to get in the car, but I refused. He grabbed me by the arm and said, "get your ass in the car." During this time, the dealer showed up and went inside the house. Seeing that dealer made me want the drug even more. At that moment, nothing else mattered. I remember telling Will that it would do no good if I left with him now. I would go when I got the chance because I was not yet done getting high. Like I said earlier, I was what you call a binge smoker. Binging is "using as much crack cocaine as I can until I run out of crack or cannot think of any way to use any more. By the time I was done binging anywhere from three to seven days, I would be so burnt out that I would be abstinent few weeks.

Will finally gave up trying to convince me to get into the car and said, "I am going to sit here with you while you get high. I was like, okay, let us get in there before this dealer leaves. Once we got the drugs, the dealer left, and the girl and I took a hit of the crack. Will was sitting at the table with us when he said give me a hit. Instantly I sobered up and said no, let us leave now. I am done. By this time, Will had already been triggered and was ready to indulge. The table had turned when he asked for a hit reality set in for me, and I knew this would destroy the both of us. Thinking back at all my past relationships, I was seen as the screw-up, and I was okay with that. But my men had always been what you call sober-minded and levelheaded. So, we sat there and smoked crack all night long. We got to know a different side of each other that we never imagined was there. This loving relationship we had would slowly turn into an unhealthy co-dependent relationship.

After that night, I was so apologetic because if I had not relapsed first, he probably would not have. He forgave me because he understood addiction, although he did not know how I gave in when we were happy and in love. We vowed not to use it again, and we were able to stick to it for a few weeks. One Friday after work, he came home and said, "I feel like getting something," which meant he wanted to get high. I quickly responded okay. So, we went back to that girl's house and sat there all-night smoking crack. We did not think about how much money he was spending because I still had money left from my settlement. Not long after, we began smoking during the week. In the beginning, Will was able to go to work after being up all night slowly; he began calling in. One day his job was doing random Urinalysis, so Will came clean with Human Resources and asked for treatment. He was put on a thirty-day medical leave and was expected to complete SUD treatment during that time. But that did not happen. During the next month, we smoked crack almost daily, spending the remainder of my settlement money.

Two days before his thirty-day leave was over; Will planned to enter treatment. I dropped him off in Tacoma at a facility before he got out of the car, and we took a hit in the parking lot. Two days later, he called and asked me to pick him up because his job had fired him for not utilizing his leave for treatment. I picked him up we spent the last of the money on crack. Will was able to get unemployment that lasted for six months. During this time, my teenage daughters were spending most weekends at their sister's house, who also lived in Auburn. The weekend is when we would get high because unemployment checks came on Thursdays. We had stopped going to Church, and our relationship turned into something very unhealthy for the both of us. We had love for each other, but drugs seem to have become the head of our lives. Most heavy users have one great love: their addiction. The more we got into drugs, the more time and effort we put into feeding our addiction. Life became a rollercoaster ride: finding drugs, using them, and figuring out how to get money to use more. The love we once showed to each other became second place; feeding our addiction was first. Crack became our idol. We no longer worshipped God, we replaced Him for crack, who became the head of our lives and kept us in the dark. Romans 1:21-25 says, "For although they knew God, they did not honor him as God or give thanks to him, but they became futile in their thinking, and their foolish hearts were darkened... Claiming to be wise, they became fools and exchanged the glory of the immortal God for images resembling mortal man, birds, animals, and reptiles. They exchanged the truth about God for a lie and worshiped and served the creature rather than the Creator."

Eventually, Will found another job which slowed down our drug use because payday was every two weeks. By this time, we began using drugs at home because we did not have enough money to share with the lady down the street, which was a good thing because that lady had kids just like I did, but since she did not care about people using drugs with her kids in the house, we did not care either. That is such a sad truth to admit that I was so caught up in drugs I had no respect for those kids. We did not use it in front of them because they were made to stay in their rooms when we would come over to smoke crack. It did not matter how long we were there; those kids only came out to use the bathroom. I remember we would bring the kids McDonald's and junk food from the store to ease our consciences. I am so grateful at this moment for God forgiving me; I feel guilty as I am writing this truth.

Will and I spent another six months on a rollercoaster ride. We were only able to pay our rent because I was on the Section 8 program before we were married. This program paid most of your rent if you had a low income, which meant my rent was only two hundred dollars. When we got married, I did not report that I was married with more income. I also was receiving food stamps for my kids and me, so we were able to get by and self-destruct smoking crack. I remember we would drive down long roads where there was light traffic and smoke while driving. I remember one time we were playing a game calling out a certain car, saying it was the police. After smoking more drugs and playing this game, we became paranoid, and every car looked like it was the police.

I remember taking all the drugs and throwing them out of the window. Will was so ticked off that we ended up stopping and buying more before returning home. This is just an example of the paranoia and delusional thinking that comes with excessive drug use. When crack became our idol, we walked away from the light and opened the door to Satan and his strongholds, who gained access to our "souls (mind, will, and emotions)" We opened the door to the demonic realm, which had a stronghold on our lives we could not shake off because we kept using the drugs. I remember at the end of our drug use; we would get so paranoid in our home that we would go to a hotel room.

Earlier I said that Will and I had different patterns of smoking crack. For years I was a binger, which means I had breaks in between my use. Will could smoke daily and semi-function. Eventually, my pattern changed to his daily smoking pattern if I had it. This was when the paranoia and delusion happened more often and more intensely. I remember we spent the night at a hotel getting high. When it was close to eleven, Will kept saying come on; we got to go. I just sat there saying I am not leaving because help was on the way. I remember hoping the police would come because I was so tired of being afraid. I was tired of hearing the police outside my bedroom window. I was tired of being fearful of taking a shower because of all the voices I would hear when the water ran. I also remember driving to get drugs and listening to Gospel music, crying because I missed the peace that comes with the presence of God. I remember Will would see me crying, saying we were almost done with this mess. This is an example of how Satan can have a stronghold in our lives that seems impossible to eliminate. 2 Corinthians 10:4-5 says: We are humans, but we do not wage war as humans do. We use God's mighty weapons, not worldly weapons, to knock down the strongholds of human reasoning and to destroy false arguments. We destroy every proud obstacle that keeps people from knowing God." Strongholds are lies that become our truths, something embedded in our soul that interferes with our ability to know God.

The last few months of drug use together were chaotic; we were both a mess. We suffered from sleep deprivation and loss of appetite because we were using daily, resulting in malnutrition. My hair started thinning out, my teeth ached, and the pain in my kidneys was so intense because of dehydration. We had lost interest in other things that life had to offer. It seemed like we did not feel normal until we had a hit of crack. I remember one time we had some crack, and when it was gone, I started crying, Will felt so bad for me that he got more. How pitiful was that? Not pitiful enough because I kept on using. This is an example of how relationships become co-dependent on drug use. Like we forgot that the purpose of our union was for us to empower one another to fulfill the purpose God had planned. Instead, we had each other's back and supported each other to stay in bondage to the spirit of addiction. One night we had to walk six blocks to meet the dealer. I remember having pains near my heart with each step. But I kept the pain to myself so that I could get that crack even if I died trying. You are most likely wondering why we both did not just stop. Crack interferes with how the brain processes chemicals, making us feel we need more crack just to feel normal. Jesus said in (John 10:10)., "The thief cometh not, but for to steal, and to kill, and to destroy, but I came that they might have life and that they might have it more abundantly." The devil was attempting to destroy God's plans for our lives.

CHAPTER 13

Failed Urinalysis

*I*n February 2004, I had a severe sinus infection which led me to the emergency room. Upon discharge, I was given three prescriptions. One of the prescriptions was Oxycodone for pain. I had to wait until the next morning to fill them because the pharmacy was closed. The following morning, I had Will call the drug dealer to see if he wanted to trade the pain pills for crack. The dealer said yes, he would make the trade. The prescription was for fifteen pain pills. Before leaving for the pharmacy, I altered the prescription, changing the one to a four. I remember my youngest daughter asked whether she could go with me. I told her no because she was not ready and needed to hurry back. I dropped the prescriptions at the pharmacy and walked around the store while filling them. About twenty minutes later, I heard my name over the intercom. It was the pharmacy informing me my prescriptions were ready. Once I got to the window, the pharmacist handed me two of the prescriptions. She then said she could not fill the pain pills because the prescription had been altered. I denied altering the prescription. She responded someone did because the emergency room never writes a script for over fifteen. I said OKAY and walked out with the two that had been filled. Once outside, a police officer met me at the door. He asked my name and then said I was under arrest for attempted forgery. I was so surprised but did not resist in any way because I knew I was wrong. My second thought was, "I am so glad I told my daughter no when she asked to go with me." This all happened on a Saturday morning, so I had to sit over the weekend until Monday morning. Monday morning, a detective came and talked to me and asked what happened, and I admitted to my wrong. Her response was they would let me go because the pharmacy should not have filled any of the prescriptions. So, I was released that morning and walked home. About a month later I received a summons to go to court; there I was charged with forgery and ordered to get a drug assessment and follow the treatment recommendations.

The recommendation was for me to complete nine months of outpatient treatment. The weekend before I started treatment, Will and I got high for our supposedly last time because taking random urinalysis tests are part of outpatient treatment. The treatment center would send monthly progress reports to the court, including urinalysis results. So, I started treatment. I went three times a week in the evening; each session was three hours. One evening when I got home, I could tell that Will had been getting high. My response was, did you save me some, and he had. This was on a Thursday evening, so I was in the clear because I did not go back to treatment until Monday. My thought was the drugs would be out of my system by Monday if I did not use them after this Thursday evening. Well, we did not stop on that Thursday. We also indulged on that Sunday. Now I am scared because I know my urine would be dirty. To get out of being caught, I had my youngest daughter urinate into a cup and pour the urine into a prescription bottle. It was a Tuesday when I had to take the Urinalysis test. I was not nervous about it because I had this thirteen-year-old's urine. The Urinalysis results usually take twenty-four hours to get the results because they are sent out to a laboratory for accuracy.

Thursday, when I got to the treatment center, the Director and my counselor called me into the Director's office. They revealed that my test returned positive for cocaine, and it was a higher quantity than when I started treatment. I sat there in shock because I knew that somehow my test had to have gotten mixed up with someone else's. I could not argue that because I was fearful that they would call Child Protective Services if I told them I had involved my daughter to cover up my mess. The Director asked me whether I wanted to be clean or not. I told her the truth that my husband is also in active addiction, getting high while I am in treatment. They called my husband and scheduled a family meeting for the following day. They sat us both down and explained that they recommended I go to an inpatient treatment center called Residence X11 in Kirkland, WA. They also told him, "Your wife is trying to get her life together, but she can't do it if you don't get yours together." They recommended that Will commit to outpatient treatment while I went to inpatient. They then said if you do not want to do that, why do not you leave so your wife will have a chance. He agreed to treatment, and it felt good to know a change was coming.

A few days later, I went for an assessment at Residence X11. It was an elite private twenty-four-bed all-women's program. After the assessment, we talked to the finance department where we found out that we would have to pay a twenty-five hundred deductible at the time of admission. We told them that we did not have the money for a deductible, and we left. This meant I would not be able to get into treatment and most likely would have to go to jail for not complying with the treatment recommendations. The next morning, I received a call from the Director of Residence X11. She wanted to let me know that the board had decided to offer me a scholarship for treatment. I was so excited to be accepted, and I felt like God had just relit my candlestick, and my fire was burning once again. When I look back, God was in this from the beginning starting with the positive urinalysis, which was my ticket to treatment now a scholarship to pay for the treatment.   Sometimes when we are in the middle of sin and feel like we are so undeserving of being called a child of God because of guilt and shame, God shows up full of Grace, making a way out of no way to show us His unconditional love. Romans 5:6-8 reads, "You see, at just the right time, when we were still powerless, Christ died for the ungodly. Very rarely will anyone die for a righteous person, though someone might dare to die for a good person. But God demonstrates his own love for us in this: While we were still sinners, Christ died for us."

My treatment admission date was ten days away, so I decided to continue going to outpatient treatment and was able to stay sober. Residence X11 was an impressive program. All the counselors were in recovery and were enthusiastic about the work they were doing. During my second week there, I was pulled aside and told my insurance was not going to pay for my treatment because it was out of network. When I asked about my scholarship, it was explained the scholarship was only covering the deductible that I initially could not afford. At this time, I had five weeks clean I was disappointed that I could not stay but was feeling positive that I could return to outpatient treatment and succeed. The next day I was discharged and got home to find Will doing well in his outpatient treatment. Now we both were in treatment; I went in the morning, and Will went in the evenings after work. I had a recovery Bible that I read faithfully daily; this was the first time in eighteen months I felt the joy of the Lord, and I felt happy. One morning at the end of June, I remember Will looking at me and saying I am glad you are happy. I did not realize at that time that he was struggling to get his JOY back. This makes me think of the few times in the past when I went to treatment because it was my last resource, not because I wanted to stop. Will loved me and agreed to go to treatment because the counselors told him I could not make it if he were not trying. In recovery, there are various stages that individuals addicted go through, such as restlessness, irritability, and discontentedness due to feeling the loss of the effects of substances. If we do not fill those voids with "prayer, worship and the Word of God" we will be powerless because God is the one who empowers us to make it through the wilderness experiences. Isaiah 43:19 reads, "I will make a way in the wilderness and rivers in the desert." During wilderness experiences, we can feel like we are all alone and that there is no light at the end of the tunnel. This can cause us to want to give up and stop trusting God. But if we can learn to embrace the journey with a student's mindset, we will pass the test and come out victorious.

CHAPTER 14

The Devil Came
With A Bang

Two months into our recovery process, life took a turn for the worst. Will came home from work and said, "I want to get high" I said no, we are doing so good. It was like the tables had turned from the first time we relapsed together. This time it was me saying no, we do not need it, but he was persistent, and I gave in. We started smoking crack on a Friday evening and ended on a Sunday. It was hot outside this time, and we were cooped up in our bedroom, tripping off the sounds we heard outside. I remember early that Sunday afternoon; we were sitting out back looking towards the river. Will said I see all my people which meant he saw his family on the other side of the river. I remember saying, "you're tripping. There is nobody over there." He was persistent that they were over there; Today, I know he saw something;

maybe it was his angels preparing the way for him to go to a better place.

Once we went back inside, I realized we were out of drugs; I felt relieved because I was so done. I remember going and taking a shower, preparing to rest for the evening, and figuring out how was I going to come clean with the counselor that I had relapsed. Once I got out of the shower, I got into the bed to come down and try to relax. Our bedroom was on the bottom floor, and I could hear the neighbors outside enjoying the sunny evening. We had put a sheet over our window so we could leave it open without the neighbors looking in and hoping the smoke would not seep out. Will was not in the room, but I heard a knock at the front door. Will returned to the room with more drugs in his hand. I was upset and said to him. "I thought we were done." He responded this is it. I told him that I did not want anymore, and I was done. Before he could take a hit, we heard a big bang from the window and that sheet we had neatly laid to the side. It was like someone gently removed the sheet. We also had a screen on our window that was intact. I initially thought that one of the neighbor kids must have thrown a ball and hit our window. Will went to the window and began saying, "I see you; I see you out there. I said, "there is nobody out there. You are just tripping again; earlier that day, he said he saw his family out back. Will's demeanor changed; he sat on the edge of the bed with the pipe and drugs in his hand, looking around the room. He looked petrified; he was seeing something that I could not see. Ephesians 6:12 reads, "For we are not fighting against flesh-and-blood enemies, but against evil rulers and authorities of the unseen world, against mighty powers in this dark world, and against evil spirits in the heavenly places." He was sitting there hunched over for maybe a minute, and suddenly, he stood up with his chest out. I no longer saw fear; I saw boldness. He walked to the bathroom, and I heard the toilet flush. He walked back into the room with his head up high. I asked him whether he flushed the crack down the toilet. He said yes, I did. My addicted mind awakened, and I asked, why would you do that? He said God told me to get the devil out of you. Initially, I was not afraid; my thoughts were he has been up to long and was having a psychotic break. At this time, I was sitting on the bed, and he approached me, stating again, "God wants me to get the devil out of you." He then pulled his fist back to punch me in the face. But before reaching my face, something blocked the punch, and he began saying, "okay, okay, I can't hit my wife, but I can lay hands on her." He then took the palms of his hand and began hitting me in my forehead, kind of like when you are in an aggressive prayer at the altar where those pastors are attempting to cause you to fall under the power of the Holy Spirit. At this time, I was not yet fearful; I was in shock because physical abuse was not something that went on in our marriage. After a minute or so, he grabbed me, threw me on the floor, and said, "God told me to take your eyeballs out." Now I am afraid; I began screaming for help, I could hear people outside, but no one heard me screaming. We then began to wrestle; he attempted to pin my head under the bed frame with his hand directly on my face using his thumbs to gouge out my eyes. Will was a large man. His height was six feet two or three, and he weighed over two hundred pounds. During the wrestling, I began to scream. He said you could scream all you want no one is going to hear you, and he was right. Not sure how long this went on, but we were both dripping wet with sweat which interfered with him having the leverage he needed to gouge out my eyes. I remember becoming exhausted and dehydrated, I asked him if I could please have some water, and he yelled, "no, you cannot have any water, and no one is coming to help you." We proceeded to wrestle. I remember just moving my head back and forth; this caused his hands to continue to slip because of the sweat. Finally, I was feeling like all the fight I had was leaving. I prayed and asked God to let me please just pass out so I did not have to feel the pain of whatever he was going to do to me but what kept me going was the voices I could hear outside. My thoughts were someone must be hearing all this commotion. The last words Will said to me was, "God told me to get the devil out of you." When he said that, I opened my eyes and shouted you are the devil. When I looked into his eyes, I no longer saw Will something else had taken over and was trying to kill me. He again said, "God told me to get the devil out of you." I shouted back at him, "you are the devil, and I rebuke you in the name of Jesus." He came at me again, and one more, I yelled as loud as I could, "you are the devil, and I rebuke you in the name of Jesus." Suddenly, he said OKAY, then he backed off me and began chanting, "thank you, Jesus, thank you, Jesus, thank you, Jesus." He was lying on his back, sliding away from me, still chanting, "thank you, Jesus, thank you, Jesus." I jumped up, ran to my bedroom window, knocked down the screen, jumped out the window, and ran upstairs to my neighbors. I was yelling. "Did you not hear me yelling?" Their reply was no; we did not hear anything. I proceeded to call the police; I told them that my husband had been smoking crack all weekend and was having a psychotic break and needed to go to the hospital.

CHAPTER 15

Excessive Force

---

*P*olice arrived in about ten minutes; they asked if they could kick in my friend's door. I told them they did not need to use force; the bedroom window was open. The police report said they approached the bedroom window, and Will was standing there with his Bible in his hand. They asked him if they could talk to him, and he nodded. Once inside, the officers instructed Will to get down on the ground, but he did not comply. There were five police officers in the room with him; I could imagine him being fearful and not understanding what was going on. They instructed him to the ground again with no response from Will. Records show they tased him three times with no response from Will. They proceeded to tackle him to the ground using one of their clubs. While all this is going on inside, I am outside with the entire "cul de a-sac" watching and waiting; my neighbor's sister-in-law said I hope they do not tase him. She explained that her husband is a police officer in California, and they were warned not to tase anyone under the influence of stimulants because studies have shown it could potentially cause the individual to have a cardiac arrest. After about ten minutes, everything was quiet inside, and then I saw an ambulance at the end of the block. Another ten minutes go by before the paramedics make it down to my garage door. My garage door opens; the paramedics go in and carry my husband out, hog-tied like an animal, and place him on the gurney. The look on his face is something that I will never forget. His face appeared swollen, and his eyes were big as half dollars and bright red. The police said they were taking him to the hospital to be checked because of the tasing. Three minutes after they pull away, a police officer comes to the door and says I must leave because this is a crime scene. He said Will's heart stopped. I remember falling to the ground and yelling, "I wanted you to help him, not kill him." As soon as I got those words out, the police officer said they had revived him. I yelled, "you insensitive sons of bitches." My family is there now, and I am an emotional mess. I get to the hospital about an hour later. His youngest son was also there. The doctor explained that he had suffered a heart attack and was put into an induced coma. He also shared that his arm was so damaged and would eventually need surgery but was not optimistic that Will would ever gain much use back because of the tendon and cartilage damage that was done. I stayed at the hospital for a short while before going home to rest. Before going to bed that night, I called his sister and informed her that Will had a cardiac arrest. I also called our Pastor and informed him that Will had a heart attack. I did not give him the details; I just asked for prayer.

When I look back at the whole weekend, the true definition of spiritual warfare was a nightmare. Today I know that Will did see those evil forces at our window that day, and they came in and took over our home. Addiction begins in the spiritual realm and is authored by the devil. John 10:10 reads, "The thief's purpose is to steal, kill, and destroy. My purpose is to give them a rich and satisfying life" Brokenness and destruction are the reality of life apart from God. Once we gave in and bought that crack, we opened the door to the spiritual realm of darkness and gave the devil permission to come into our home. The devil came to destroy the little progress we had made, including our emotional wellness and our relationship, and destroy our dreams. But Jesus said again in John 10:10, "The thief cometh not, but for to steal, and to kill, and to destroy. I am come that they might have life, and that they might have it more abundantly." So, "God is our abundance" means that God makes our lives abundant and provides all of us with all that we need for our body, soul, and spirit. It took me more than two years before I could see and appreciate this beautiful gift of abundance that God had promised.

CHAPTER 16

God Called Him Home

The following day, I went to the hospital around nine in the morning. By the time I arrived, Will had been transported to a private room in the intensive care unit. The doctor came in and explained that they had attempted to bring him out of the induced coma with no success. The doctor also said that his organs had begun to shut down, giving no explanation as to why. I remember going into his room and telling him that I forgave him for yesterday; I told him he had to repent to God. I instructed him to move his fingers when he was done. Two of his fingers on that broken arm moved a few minutes later. I cried and thanked God for "His" grace. I knew in my heart that he would not make it through this, and that God was taking him home to Glory. The night before, I saw his Bible on the nightstand; it was opened to where he was reading when the police arrived. Ecclesiastes 3:1–2 reads, "There is a time for everything, and a season for every activity under the heavens: a time to be born and a time to die" In this passage, Solomon acknowledged that, from start to finish, every moment in every season of the cycle of life, is appointed by God. From the day of our birth until the day we die, God is designing our destiny. During Job's struggles, he said to God, "You have decided the length of our lives. You know how many months we will live, and we are not given a minute longer" (Job 14:5). People loosely say cliches like "it wasn't their time", and "gone too soon". The truth is God uses circumstances that we cannot understand to allow the deaths of our loved ones to happen at the precise right minute that was planned from the moment they were created. This is hard for us to accept during the early moments of grieving. The natural grieving response is to blame someone else or even ourselves.

Most of his family had arrived by the evening and were at the hospital waiting for their mother to arrive from Mississippi. I remember the doctor saying, "he is holding on for somebody." I had never met his mother or other siblings until this moment, and it was an unpleasant experience for all of us. I knew they blamed me for his relapse and his death just as I blame myself. My thoughts were if I had not used drugs first, or if I had not called the police, he would not be lying there dying. When I walked past his sons and other family members, I felt like I was taking the walk of shame. I remember going outside for air, sitting on the curb, and finally, reality hit me, and I was uncontrollably crying; shortly after, I was in the middle of a full-blown panic attack. My daughter's aunt was outside with me at the time; she ran to the hospital for help. I was taken into a room where I was given a sedative. My brother was also there in the room with me, gently rubbing my head and telling me that everything was going to be okay. A few hours later, I was woken up by the news that Will had passed on to Glory. By the time I got upstairs, most of his family had already left the hospital. I really did not feel many emotions at the time; it was kind of a relief accepting that he is at peace in a better place. God had the final say, and Will was walking in victory as I stayed here to continue to fight the battles of guilt, shame, remorse, and addiction. We were two addicts very much in love, wanting to serve God and have a normal relationship, but our addiction got in the way, so God stepped in with the final say.

Sadly, our Pastor never made it to the hospital or call to see how we were doing. I did call him to give him the news. His response was, "I didn't know it was that bad." Sadly, drug addicts sometimes get judged by the church because many there fail to understand that addiction is a sickness that starts with sin and becomes a disease of the mind (stronghold). "Is anyone among you in trouble? Let them pray. Is anyone happy? Let them sing songs of praise. Is anyone among you sick? Let them call the church elders to pray over them and anoint them with oil in the name of the Lord. And the prayer offered in faith will make the sick person well; the Lord will raise them. If they have sinned, they will be forgiven."

The following day his family came to my home for a meeting; they wanted to ask me if they could take Will's body back to Mississippi to be buried. I remember feeling so awkward in my own home with all these angry and grieving people. Because of their anger toward me, they could not show me any compassion for my loss. My decision was to lay him to rest here in Washington. Later that evening, his best friend called and pleaded with me to allow his mother permission so they could have a funeral in his hometown. I stuck to my original decision, which I can admit was selfish at the time. But I know Will hated Mississippi; he experienced a lot of unfair treatment being raised down south in the sixties. Today I know it was the right decision because his youngest son lives here in Washington, and I am certain he visits his dad's gravesite when he needs to feel a little closer to his dad. I received a call the following day from Will's employer informing me that Will had a twenty-five-thousand-dollar life insurance policy along with his final paycheck. I was so relieved because now I did not have to depend on anyone else to give him a proper home-going. He also served four years in the military, meaning his gravesite and burial were already taken care of. The funeral home made all the arrangements on consignment, meaning I did not have to worry about paying upfront because they knew I had a life insurance policy. The day of the funeral was a sad day not only because we were saying goodbye but because our families were divided. His family sat on one side, and my family and friends were on the other side. Our Pastor officiated the funeral, which was beautiful because he knew what an impressive man Will was before our fall.

The day after the funeral, detectives began showing up at my door, investigating Will's death due to the Auburn police being involved. They interviewed all the neighbors; they were getting their stories together to show justification for the force they used. One neighbor across from us reported seeing the whole thing because he could see directly into our bedroom from his balcony. He said that Will was just standing there, and the police came in forcefully, not giving him a chance to comply. I imagine the fear and confusion he must have felt because he had just been through this spiritual battle which I do not believe he was aware of the natural. I also was on the news sharing the events of that day. Attorneys called wanting to meet with me to see if there was a case against the police department. It was all very overwhelming, I tried to keep it together, but I had moments where I could not manage the reality of his death. I was mad not at God but at the situation, meaning God took him to Glory, and I was still here to continue the struggle of addiction and the aftermath of the events that led to his death. I played over and over in my mind that day and regretted choosing to call the police. I could have just left for the rest of the day, and maybe he would still be alive. Today I know it is not true; life happens the way it is supposed to happen; even if it does not make sense, we must trust God through the process. God always has the final say. This includes the day and time each of us will take our last breaths.

For the next five months, I continued to smoke crack, not as much or as often as I had before his death, but enough to keep my life in a dismantled state. During this time, my mother was diagnosed with stage four lung cancer. I remember being in the doctor's office when he gave us the results from her MRI. I walked out of that office full of tears. I prayed to God and asked him to keep her alive until I get my life together because I did not want her last thoughts of me to be anything but good. I remember she called me at about six in the morning after she started chemo, asking me to come over for coffee. She never called, so I hurried up and headed to her apartment. When I arrived, she was tearful because her hair had begun to fall out due to the treatments. I am so grateful I was not up to getting high so I could be there for her in such a devastating time. My personal life was devastating as well, I had sold most of what was valuable in my home. My computer, one of my televisions, nice lamps, and whatever else worth any value I could trade for drugs. My second youngest daughter was living with my oldest daughter; my youngest daughter stayed with me part of the time and my second oldest daughter part-time. I am so grateful for my family stepping in and taking on my responsibilities as a parent when I could not give them the love and care they deserved.

CHAPTER 17

Second Suicide Attempt

*D*uring this time, I felt so lost and guilty about Will's death that I wanted to die. I decided I wanted to have a cardiac arrest like Will because I felt lost without him. I bought some crack and got a hotel room not far from my house. I knew I wanted to die but did not want my kids to live with the horror of finding me dead with a crack pipe in my hand. Again, my motive was not to get high. It was to die. I got to the room in the late evening. I had maybe one hundred dollars' worth of crack. I began putting big hits of crack on the pipe and holding it in as long as possible before exhaling. I thought that my heart would explode if I did this long enough. All night long, I would put a hit on hold my breath, exhale, and then cry because I was still alive. I remember it was around nine in the morning, and I was still alive. I had until eleven to get the job done. I thought I would go into cardiac arrest, the housekeepers would find me, and my misery would be over. I even prayed to God that if it were not my time to die, would He please allow me to go into a coma and become a new person. I know this sounds crazy, but this is what depression mixed with low self-worth and addiction looks like. This is how the father of lies consumes our minds when we choose to sin deliberately. I put the remainder of the crack on my pipe and sucked it in as slowly as possible. I remember I felt a burning sensation in my lungs; I thought it was working.

I blew the smoke out, and instantly my feet went limp; I passed out and entered a spiritual realm. I began hearing a voice; it felt like a few people around me were deciding if I should live or die. One of the voices said, "look at her. She looks so peaceful now" I heard another voice saying, "Tammie, it's not your time yet; you have to breathe" I then heard a third voice saying, "but she looks so peaceful." Then I heard a familiar voice; it was my ex-husband's voice. He was saying in a stern voice, Tammie you must breathe; his voice then yelled at me, "Got dammed, Tammie you better breathe right now." I gasped for air, opened my eyes, and realized I was in this room all alone, and I was alive. I lay there and cried like a baby. I then looked at the time, which was ten minutes to eleven. I jumped up, cleaned up my mess, and headed out the door. When I opened the door, there was a housekeeper across the hall. She looked at me with the warmest smile, saying good to see you breathing. To this day I believe the housekeeper was one of my guardian angels assigned by God. I know that some are thinking, how selfish? How could you think your family would be better off without you? The truth is when a person feels hopeless and their life has no value, it makes sense to them the moment they choose to take their own life.

Reliving this experience through my writing is how I produced the title for this memoir. Tasha Cobb has a song called" Never Gave Up on Me." The song is about how patient God is and how He never gives up on us even in our times of depression and despair. One verse says, "I was depressed and wounded, helpless but then you called me by name begging me to come, you gave me living water, you covered me with love and silenced the shame, you kept your arms wide open and never gave up on me waiting patiently. God had so many reasons to give up on me. That morning in that Hotel, God called me by name using a voice that I trusted, I was at the end of the road, but God said I have more in store for you, and you will win this battle because "I crowned you before I cleaned you."

CHAPTER 18

Diligently Seeking God

y life was a total mess. I wanted to stop this destructive lifestyle of mine but had no strength to do it on my own. December 2004, I was so depressed that I turned on the TBN Christian channel. The Pastor speaking was teaching on fasting and the importance of starting the new year with fresh revelations from God. At that moment, I heard God speaking so; clearly, He said, "daughter go on a ten-day fast, and I'll meet you there." I remember feeling this formidable unexplainable presence, and I said yes, I am going on a fast; I planned to start a liquid fast on December twenty-sixth. The fast consisted of only broth and water for ten days, along with prayer, worship, and reading the Word of God. I started the fast as planned; the first day was tough the following days became easier, filled with the presence of God. It was like God kept the devil from sending people my way, tempting me to smoke crack with them. Each day I became more drawn to the word of

God because not only was I reading the Word, but I was also gaining revelation after revelation, which kept me wanting increasingly more. I remember the fifth day of the fast. I was in my garage praising God with prayer and worship music while smoking a cigarette. Yes, I was smoking; I had not been delivered yet. God meets us where we are with the intention of lifting us up when we are down.

While I was smoking and worshipping, I heard God say go out front. I remember tears rolling down my face because I was in the glory of God; it was that still, soft voice I had heard people talk about. I went out to my front porch and re-lit my cigarette. Suddenly this flock of crows came toward my house; there had to be about a hundred at least. When those birds reached my yard, those black crows turned as white as doves. I remember having this overwhelming sense of joy come over me; I quickly threw my cigarette on the grown and began crying and praying in the Spirit. At that moment, I knew God was showing me His Glory. I had a true glimpse of heaven. We imagine heaven as a place white as snow and full of purity, which is what I saw when those crows turned white as doves. "Isaiah says in Chapter 1:18, "Come now let us settle the matter," the Lord says. "Though your sins are like scarlet, they shall be white as snow; though they are red as crimson, they shall be like wool."

The next five days were impressive and powerful; I was no longer getting hungry for food because I stayed full, digesting the Word of God. I remember day seven of the fast I had this desire to cook for my neighbor upstairs. "God was transforming my heart to serve others." By Day ten was finally here; I was becoming exhausted because I had been faithful; I did not cheat—I stayed true to my commitment to fast consuming no solid foods. I remember it was around six in the evening; my fast was scheduled to end at seven. I decided to soak in the tub with a candle, worship music, and midnight blue Calgon. I filled the tub with water and poured the entire box into the tub. While in the tub listening to worship and enjoying the presence of God, I began feeling extremely hot, so I sat up with my face down, looking at the blue water. Suddenly the midnight blue water began to look like clouds. It was snow white. Instantly tears began rolling down my face. I turned my head toward the left and saw a silhouette on the side of the tub. There was also a shadow that appeared to be someone looking at me. I then heard these words "Well Done" I cried so hard and jumped out of the tub praising and praying in tongues. God was there. He was letting me know he was so proud of me. I was on a natural high for at least six months. During this time, Will's brother called me and asked if I knew where he could get some crack; I quickly replied I did not have any contacts because I had quit smoking crack. This shows the power of the disease of addiction; he was able to put his feelings about me aside if I could get him the drug he was craving at that moment. I am so grateful that I was able to say no at that moment. That is an example of passing a test and not giving in to temptation. I also attended church faithfully, strengthening my armor against the devil's schemes. God was giving me time to grow in His promises before I would experience another dark season that almost took me out spiritually, mentally, emotionally, and physically.

During the next six months, I stayed clean and focused on growing in God by reading the Bible and going to church regularly. God gave me a revelation about what happened the day trauma hit my home. If you remember me saying that Will saw something that I could not see, this was a true statement. The supernatural was in our home, which consisted of demons and assigned angels. Some call it a demonic phenomenon. Demons were there to kill and destroy the angels were there to protect. When we hear supernatural, we tend to think about God but not always so (supernatural is an existence beyond the visible observable universe). Although it appeared that Will was the target, not, so it was me that the devil was after.

Job 2:6 reads, "And the LORD said to Satan, Behold, he is in your hand, but spare his life. Luke 10:19 reads, "I have given you authority to trample on snakes and scorpions and to overcome the power of the enemy; nothing will harm you." God spared my life and showed me the authority I have in the name of Jesus.

The more I studied, the more I recognized how Satan had been trying to finish the job of destroying my life. Demons can cause thoughts of suicide (Mark 9:22), make a person sick or weak, even blind, deaf, and/or dumb

(Luke 13:11/Matthew 12:22). They can cause insanity (Matthew 17:15). Demons are fallen angels and disembodied spirits associated with Satan and rebelling against God. God showed me that when we started using drugs, we gave demons access to torment our lives, mainly in these three areas. The way to stop him in his tracks was to stay clear of sin and commit my ways to the ways of the Lord. God began showing me my spiritual Gifts. He anointed me with revelation gifts; the word of knowledge was one of the gifts. I remember going to a small storefront church for a revival. The church had no fire, but I just closed my eyes and worshipped God like I had been doing in the privacy of my home. Suddenly as I was worshipping God with my eyes closed, I began speaking uncontrollably in the Spirit, meaning I was praying in tongues. I heard someone yell it is a prophetic word which at the time, I did not understand what was happening; I was just allowing the Holy Spirit to have His way. 1Corinthians 14:27-28 reads, "If anyone speaks in a tongue, two, or at most three, should speak in turn, and someone must interpret. But if there is no interpreter, he should remain silent in the church and speak only to himself and God..."

I opened my eyes, and God moved me to the front of the church, pacing back and forth. Finally, I stopped right in front of this man, who I found out later was the speaker for the night. While in front of this man, I continued to pray in the Spirit, and God used me to interpret my own tongues. The word was "before the message is given, you must repent." The man jumped up and yelled to the congregation, "God wants us all to repent." I remember the Holy Spirit was so grieved. The words "oh no" came out of my mouth, and tears rolled down my cheeks. I went to a corner and began sobbing and praying in the Spirit. After everyone settled down, they introduced the speaker for the night, and it was the gentleman God had instructed to repent. After the service, people sat around me saying, "I want to be near the anointing." I was still in awe of what happened that night. I know it was nothing I could do in the natural world; it was all God. At that moment, God saw a need and used me with His supernatural gift that was provided at the time to instruct this man to clean the speck out of his own eye before preaching to the crowd. I believe this night, he also imparted the gift of discerning spirits. I began to experience unusual manifestations of dark spirits in the church and out of the church. For example, I was visiting a church, and my focus stayed on the organ player. His face appeared distorted, and I saw a spirit all over him. I was shocked and felt somewhat fearful because I did not understand what I saw. I told the lady I was with what I was seeing, and her response was I did not see anything. When the Pastor got up to speak, that organ player came and sat right behind me. It was like Lucifer was letting me know that he knew I could see him. I felt so uncomfortable with his presence that I got up and left the service. I began researching and discovered that I most likely was anointed with the spiritual gift of discernment. Individuals with this gift begin to see or feel things others are unaware of. These unusual sensations alert them to what is happening in the spiritual realm. Please do not take this as if I am judging the church. God was teaching me that demons are everywhere, and so many believers live a lifestyle that opens the door to demonic activity in their lives.

Another example: My old high-school friend invited me to her church for an Easter service. I arrived before her, so I got us a seat and waited. She arrived with a lady she had also invited. My friend sat next to me, and the lady sat on the other side of my friend. While the Pastor delivered the message, I experienced this unusual, uncomfortable feeling. I looked over at my friend; all I could see was a snake coming out of the face of her other guest, and I was speechless. I must have looked terrified because my friend whispered, "do you see something?" I nodded yes and attempted to listen to the sermon, but that demon stared at me the entire service. Today I know God was preparing me for the spiritual battles I would soon face. 1 Cor. 12:7-11 reads, "Now to each one the manifestation of the Spirit is given for the common good… to another gifts of healing by that one Spirit, to another miraculous powers, to another prophecy, to another distinguishing between spirits…All these are the work of one and the same Spirit, and he gives them to each one, just as he determines."

CHAPTER 19

Failed Test

inally, six months later, I received the money from my husband's life insurance policy. It took so long because there was a hold on the death certificate due to the police investigation; I was waiting for the cause of death confirmation. I learned so much about God through this season. I learned that He meets us right where we are when we diligently seek Him, through fasting and prayer. God also has our best interest at heart and knows the best time to answer our prayers.

With the insurance money in hand, I relocated, hoping to have a fresh start. I was not prepared for the spiritual warfare that I would endure before true deliverance would take place. I moved to Federal Way with my two daughters. My youngest daughter came on the weekends because she did not want to switch schools. Everything was going well for the first couple of months. I watched my girl Joyce Meyer every morning; she was so inspiring to me at that time in my life. She was so open about her years of sexual abuse; she gave me hope that I would someday share my story without feeling guilt or shame. I bought her book titled the "Battlefield of the Mind," which played a big part in my journey to freedom from my past abuse. I also was reading a book called "The Bondage Breaker" by Neil Anderson. This book was about spiritual warfare and how to break the strongholds of your life. I remember someone saying to me, "you're focusing too much on the devil." 1 Peter 5:8 reads (Be sober-minded; be watchful. Your adversary, the devil, prowls around like a roaring lion, seeking someone to devour).

Ephesians 6:12 reads, (for we do not wrestle against flesh and blood, but against the rulers, against the authorities, against the cosmic powers over this present darkness, against the spiritual forces of evil in the heavenly places). For me to win the battle, I had to understand how the devil operated and what I needed to do to break the chains off my life. I wanted so badly to walk in total freedom from addiction, unforgiveness, and bitterness.

Spiritually I was growing. I started each day with God and ended with the Word of God. I would sit on my balcony in the mornings with a cup of coffee and my bible. Across from my house was an electrical pole where a dove would be sitting. The dove's presence reminded me of the experience I had six months earlier when I was on the ten days fast, and all those crows turned white as doves. Matthew 3:16-17 reads. "As soon as Jesus was baptized, He went up out of the water. At that moment, heaven was opened, and he saw the Spirit of God descending like a dove and alighting on Him. And a voice from heaven said, "This is my Son, whom I love; with him, I am well pleased."

I obtained an attorney to represent me at the inquest during this time. An inquest is an open, public administrative hearing in which the County Coroner gathers information about suspicious deaths. This was mandatory since the police participated in Will's death. The main purpose was to see if the police would be found to be at fault in his death. We had two witnesses lined up, but on the day of the hearing, when they were crossed examined, they said, "we did not see nothing." One of the witnesses was the neighbor that said on the police report that Will did not do anything, and the police just began tasing him. This experience was so hard for me; I had to sit in that courtroom and listen to each officer share their accounts of what happened that day. On the third day, I testified to why I called the police and what I recollected happened once they arrived. I remember some of the jurors looking my way with empathy and sadness in their eyes for what I had been through and what I had to relive in that courtroom. On the third day, the County Coroner testified on his findings. He testified that if Will had not been high on a stimulant, he most likely would not have had a cardiac arrest. He then added if Will had not been tasered while high on a stimulant, most likely, he would not have suffered a cardiac arrest. After the Coroners testimony, we ended the day.

That evening when I returned, I walked to the Seven Eleven down the street. When I was leaving the store, a man I used to buy drugs got my attention by saying, "good evening, Tammie." He then went on to say he lives in the area. I responded by saying I had just moved a few blocks away. Before we parted ways, he said. "If you need anything, give me a call." Instead of me saying I am in church now, I said OKAY, thanks, I will. Within a few hours, I called him up, and he delivered me some drugs. I cannot explain to you why I gave in to my flesh so easily. I stayed up most of the night feeling numb and ashamed that I had allowed myself to slip back when it was so crucial that I show up to the courthouse with my head up high, hoping for accountability and justice for my husband. The next morning, I decided not to show up for court to hear the jury's findings. My attorney called me after the hearing asking me what happened. I told him it was to be upsetting for me to sit and watch these people stare at me and pass judgment on Will because of his drug use. He shared the verdict that no one was at fault for his death. Both parties played a part, so no one was at fault. My attorney then said it is over; you can now move on. I thanked him for representing me at no cost, and we hung up. About a week later, I received a call from the attorney, and he said he could not just let it go without at least filing a civil suit against the Auburn police department. He said the process could take about six months, and again he would take it on pro-bono. It would be five months before I would hear from him again. During the five months of waiting, I continued to stay high on crack, using the remainder of the insurance money.

I ended up worse than before my encounter with God when I heard those words, "WELL DONE." I had opened the door to the devil, and he planted himself in my mind with the intent to stop me from moving forward. If you can recall from an earlier reading, I talked about being gifted with the discerning of spirits. Once I began using crack again, I began experiencing secrecy, isolation, and intense delusions. I struggled to discern between the natural and the spiritual; this is referred to as "spiritual warfare." I was in such a dark place that I felt as though I was being held captive by heavy chains. When I would sit on my balcony with coffee in hand, I no longer saw the dove on the power line; it was replaced with a crow. I had lost sight of the light, and now crack once again had become my idol. 1 Peter 5:8 reads, "Be sober-minded; be watchful. Your adversary, the devil prowls around like a roaring lion, seeking someone to devour." Sober-minded means that we do not allow ourselves to be captivated by any type of influence that would lead us away from sound judgment. The sober-minded individual is not "intoxicated," figuratively speaking, and is therefore calm under pressure, self-controlled in all areas, and rational. (https://www.gotquestions.org/sober-minded.html).

I was far from sober-minded—I just gave in to my addiction and let it have the best of me. I was not using many drugs during this time, but enough for the enemy to stay rooted in my mind. During this time, I met this guy while I was out walking; he asked did I know where He could get some crack. I got the crack for him, and he came back to my place to smoke. He stopped by the next evening and the next evening; it came to be a nightly routine. One evening he stopped by, I asked him if he had a place to live, and he responded that he did not. I told him that he could sleep on my couch at night, but he had to leave first thing in the morning. This went on for about a week until he decided he would not leave one morning. At about seven in the morning, I heard my front door shut, assuming he had left. After showering for the day, I opened my bedroom closet to find something to wear and screamed. That man did not leave he was sleeping in my closet. I was so upset that I told him to leave and never return, and he left his bag with his personal items inside. Three days after he had left, he gave me a call around nine in the evening. He asked whether I would bring his bag down to an apartment that was a floor below me. I said sure; I also brought my crack pipe just in case he had some drugs. I got to the apartment, he opened the door, let me in, and quickly shut the door behind me. Once inside, I realized nobody lived there; it was an empty apartment into which he had broken. He had a hold of my shirt; I thought he would rape me. But that did not happen; he just kept a grip on me and walked around room-to-room, mumbling. My first feeling was fear, fear of the unknown.

But as time passed, the fear turned to anger, and I wanted out of there. Finally, I started praying real low in the Spirit, suddenly, I could hear my prayers getting louder, and I was praying in the Spirit, tongues. I yanked my arm from him and continued to pray. I convinced him to let me leave; once I got to my apartment, I called the police. To make a long story short, the man had just been released from prison a few months before I met him. He served thirteen years for holding his ex-wife and kids' hostage for three days. The police could trace what apartment he was in from my phone records because he had called me from another apartment once he noticed the police outside. There was a 12-hour standoff before he was shot and died at the scene. God has protected me from evil for the fourth time thus far: Psalm 32:7 reads, "You are a hiding place for me; You preserve me from trouble; You surround me with shouts of deliverance. Selah"

After this event, I heard jokes like, "Don't mess with Tammie, or you won't make it out alive." I also received inspiring comments, like, "God is protecting you because he will use you to help others through your testimony. This was when I began to understand that I was something special to God, and even with my sinful, dirty lifestyle, God saw it fit to crown me as His child. Unfortunately, even though I was something special, I still had to suffer the consequences of my choice to entertain darkness.

CHAPTER 20

Another Psychosis Experience

fter that day, I decided not to allow anyone to come to my home. I was still using drugs but not as often. One evening an old associate of Will's who we would get drugs from called me and said he had a guy at his home spending a lot of money on crack and asked if I wanted to come by and smoke with the guy. I was initially hesitant because I had been assaulted years ago after smoking with a man who expected sex once the drugs were gone. He said no, it is not that kind of party. The guy just wanted someone to get high with because he was getting paranoid smoking all alone. I said sure and drove down to his house, where he sat all night getting high. If you remember, I was a binger, so I asked the dealer whether he knew anyone who wanted to buy a car. He found a buyer. Mind you; I just paid four thousand dollars for my car with the life insurance money. Four months later, I sold it for two thousand.

I bought maybe four hundred dollars' worth of crack and had the dealer drop me off at home. During this time, I was living alone in my apartment. My two daughters were staying with their sister in Kent. By this time, I had been up more than twenty-four hours and had all these drugs. I remember going to the store to buy myself a pack of cigarettes and a bottle of wine. It had to be maybe three in the afternoon, it was springtime, so I opened the curtains, cracked the windows, and started smoking crack in the living room. I lived on the third floor, so I did not have to worry about anyone looking in my window. Before I knew it, hours had passed by, and it was getting dark outside. I began feeling very paranoid; I began seeing a dark figure sitting on my patio. I got up and went to the patio and opened the curtain; nothing was there. I turned on the balcony light so I could see more clearly. Once I returned to the couch and looked toward the balcony, that figure was there again. It looked like the figure was wearing a spider man suit, but it was all black. I got up again and opened the balcony door, which had disappeared. Finally, I realized this was a spirit tormenting me. I began talking to it: I said I know you are trying to mess up my high, but it is not going to work, and I hit the pipe. Once I acknowledged that I knew what it was, a spirit trying to torment me, it disappeared. Around eleven at night, I began hearing these creepy noises in my kitchen. I would get up and go to the kitchen, and nothing would be there. Mentally and physically, I was drained and tired of feeling paranoid. I had about fifty dollars' worth of crack left, so I decided to go to my bedroom, smoke the rest, and call it a night. I turned off all the lights in the front of the apartment and headed to my bedroom in the back. I decided to pack my pipe with the rest of the crack so I could be done with it. I did think that this could possibly explode my heart, but my thoughts were, "I hope it does." My delusional thought was death is freedom, I cannot get this God thing right, I suck as a daughter and mother, my husband is dead because of me, so what is the point of living. I packed the pipe with the remaining crack. While I was hitting the pipe, all I could hear was snap, crackle, pop. It sounded like firecrackers going off on the fourth of July. I held in the smoke for as long as possible, hoping my heart would explode. As soon as I blew it out, I heard someone running down my hallway. Its male voice said, "Get her, bite her in the face." I began screaming at the top of my lungs and covered my head with my covers. It sounded like dogs were trampling around my room. I heard the male's voice again, commanding the dogs to bite me in the face. I was screaming at the top of my lungs. I am not sure how long this went on, but I know that there were moments when I attempted to calm myself down by telling myself that I was just tripping out. But when I would calm down, I could feel the dog's breath on my face, and then I would begin screaming again. It is astounding to me that I lived in an apartment, and it was late at night; neighbors had to have heard something, but no one responded. It reminded me of when Will attacked me, and no one heard my screams. Then through the horror, I heard my phone ringing, but I could not move because I was too afraid to move. But then, suddenly, a peaceful feeling came over me, and everything was silent. Momentarily my phone began ringing again; I jumped up and answered it. I heard my second oldest daughter on the other line asking me, "mom is everything you okay" I yelled no, I am not okay. The devil is in my house trying to kill me. My daughter said, "mom, I will call you back." My daughter called back and asked if I wanted to go to the hospital. I responded, "I don't care where I go; I have to get out of here because the devil is trying to kill me." She had called the hospital when she hung from me the first call and explained to them that I had been doing drugs and was now afraid that the devil was in my home. The hospital explained to my daughter that I was having severe psychosis and needed to come to the hospital.

We get to the hospital, and I sit in a hall while my two daughters talk to the nurse. The nurse called me to the window and asked me a few questions; while she was talking to me, I noticed the waiting area with people sitting and waiting. I leaned toward the nurse and whispered to her; I said I could not go into that room with the other people because the devil was at my house, and those people might be part of his scheme to kill me. The nurse reassured me that I would not have to go into that room. Shortly after, they took me to an exam room, gave me a gown to change into, and prepared me for an x-ray of the contusion on my forehead. Without me knowing it, I must have banged my head on my headboard while screaming in terror to get free from the spiritual attack I was experiencing. My daughter later told me that the medical staff had to put me in restraints and sedated me because I was combative. I remember the next morning, a social worker came to me and asked if I would want to go to the University of Washington for a few days so I could rest. My response was I do not care where I go because the devil is at my house, and he is trying to kill me. I was taken by ambulance to the hospital, where I spent nine days on the psychiatric floor. I would pace around for hours at a time. I was prescribed medications, but I refused to take them. Finally, one of the nurses pleaded with me to take something that would help me relax and get much-needed sleep. The next morning, the psychiatrist met with me for maybe an hour. He asked what happened that brought me to the hospital during that time. After I explained the events to him, he began explaining that I had experienced psychotic delusions and that my encounter with the devil was not real; it was a delusion. I got so upset and demanded to speak to someone spiritual like a Chaplain or Pastor.

The next morning the hospital Chaplain came to see me. We went into a small quiet room, and he asked me to share with him what happened that night—I was admitted. I explained to him about my drug use and the demonic activity that went on in my home. The Chaplain sat across from me and actively listened to me. At one point, he was tearful and asked me whether it was all right if he told me the truth about what I had experienced. I said, yes, please do. He explained to me that I got a taste of hell. He explained that hell is tormenting, and when a person is in hell, they will scream for help, but it will be too late. He then said, Tammie, you must stop doing those drugs, or you are going to end up in hell. He then prayed for me and asked whether I understood what he said. I responded, yes, I understand.

When that Chaplain left, he took every weight I was carrying with him. The next day my two older daughters arrived at the hospital for a family meeting. They asked my daughters questions about my personality and behaviors. That same day I was given a mental health diagnosis called Schizophrenia because I presented with psychosis. Psychosis is when people lose some contact with reality. This might involve seeing things that other people cannot see or hear (hallucinations) and believing things that are not actually true (delusions). Today I work in the behavioral health field, and I can tell you I was misdiagnosed. The diagnosis should have been Drug-induced Psychosis. The mental health staff made an error by disregarding my spiritual beliefs, and what the experience meant to me as a Christian.

"Making some sense of psychosis: The language and form of spirituality and religion are endemic in expressions of psychosis, even for the non-religious; meaning and purpose become distorted in psychosis with the loss of a coherent narrative. So how do we make sense of delusions, and whose intentions count? "Do we follow the psychiatrists who see religious or spiritual explanations as delusional ideas attributable to the illness, serving simply as one of its more characteristic symptoms, or do we continue to attend to the person trying to make sense of his or her or her experiences?" (Roe & Davidson 2005). John 10:10 clearly states that the devil plans to hinder, discourage and bring forth harm and destruction to us. But the good news is that we have a weapon far greater than the forces of evil, the sword, the Word of God (2 Corinthians 10:4). This tells me that spiritual warfare is real, and I was in a battle to regain my sanity and the only way this could happen for me was through deliverance and healing.

I finally was released from the hospital nine days later with a mental health diagnosis and a prescription called Lithium, usually given to individuals with bipolar or severe depression. When I got home from the hospital, I tossed the pills in the garbage because I knew it was spiritual warfare caused by my continued drug binging that brought on the psychosis. I used the last of the insurance money and booked a flight to North Carolina to a Joyce Meyer women's retreat. Once in North Carolina, I called a cab to a hotel where I met a lady who was also going to the conference; she offered me a ride both days. Once home, I felt rejuvenated; I stayed clean for two months before getting a phone call from a lady wanting to stop by and share her crack with me. Without any thought of the consequences, I said yes, come by. The next morning after she left, I remember crying and asking God why he kept testing me with drugs. God said to me, "if you learn to say no, I will do the rest." That sounded simple, but I did not know how to say no to temptation.

During this time, neither of my younger daughters were staying with me, which meant my child support had been transferred to my daughter without me knowing it. Now, I had no income source and was being evicted from my apartment. I gave all my furniture and whatever else I could not carry with me. I went to stay with my oldest daughter. She did not mind me being there if I was not using drugs in her house. I was like her house servant, I cooked and cleaned, which was a tremendous help to her, and I was earning my keep.

One weekend I decided to go over to an associate's house in West Seattle to see if they were getting high, and they were. I sat there till morning. Once I left to catch the bus home, I decided to go to the ER instead because I was feeling really depressed, and I knew that it was a waste of time to attempt suicide because it had not worked in the past. I called a cab to take me to the nearest hospital, once we got to the hospital, I apologized to the cab driver and told him I did not have any money. He was mad and yelling at me, but I just kept walking into the ER. I told the nurse that I had been using drugs all night and had a history of suicide attempts. They quickly took me back to the room and administered an IV because my blood pressure was high, and I was dehydrated. While I was lying there, two police officers came in and verbally arrested me for theft because I did not pay for the taxi. Two hours later, a social worker came in and asked if I wanted to go to detox; I said yes. It took hours for them to find an available bed, but finally, they found one way in Everett, which was an hour away. I called a friend, and she made plans to get me there. While I was there, a gentleman that was also detoxing told me about a new woman's shelter that had just opened in Everett; it was part of the Gospel Mission. I decided to call the shelter; I explained I was in detox and needed a fresh start. They gave me an appointment three days later. When I left detox, I caught the bus back to Kent, where my daughter lived and called the shelter. They instructed me to show up the following morning, so I got a bag of clothes together and caught the bus to the shelter in Everett.

CHAPTER 21

Morning Meditation

The shelter was very nice, not what you see on television. It was set up like a dorm with two bunk beds in each room. There were two full bathrooms on each floor. There was also a big, shared kitchen where you could prepare your own meals. They also had another building where the women stayed that were in the transitional program. This program was designed for women who were working and could pay $250 monthly for rent. In this building was also the main kitchen where lunch and dinner were prepared for all residents of the shelter. One of the requirements to stay at the shelter was attending meditation daily. Meditation was offered once in the morning and in the evening. This was a Christian program, so the meditations were more like a worship/ bible study service. I stayed at this shelter for four months, and not once did I crave drugs or alcohol. I became close with a few of the ladies there; we had a lot in common. We all were running to safety from self-destruction and building our personal relationships with God and needed some sort of normalcy in our lives. I had no income, so I applied for food stamps and worked through labor ready twice a week. I felt like I was free. I was being filled with the presence of God daily and he was using me to empower some of the ladies who were struggling in their faith. Two months after I arrived at the shelter, four of us ladies from the shelter went to a women's prophetic service. We arrived early so we could talk with the speakers seated at a table near the altar. There were maybe a dozen ladies there; we were all standing in line waiting our turn to hear a word from God. Finally, was my turn. I walked up to the table, and I heard the pastor say, "I don't know who you are, but God wants you to know you are full of his power; God says don't stress yourself about trying to quote scripture; you have hidden manna, His Word is stored in your heart and when it's needed God will bring it to your remembrance." I had tears flowing down my face because I had tried so hard to quote scripture but struggled due to years of drug use. (Drug use can cause brain damage and memory loss, and this damage is sometimes permanent.) After receiving this prophetic word, reading the Bible became less stressful, meaning I could soak up the Word knowing that it was stored in my heart. So, God says, I will make a new covenant to address that problem. When God comes to establish his kingdom, this will happen on that day. "I will put my law within them, and I will write it on their hearts; and I will be their God, and they shall be my people, and (Jeremiah 31:33). After this event, I dove harder into the Word of God; it seemed more manageable for me to understand the Word without the expectation that I had to quote it to be a faithful Christian. The shelter was a busy place. Twenty women were living in our dorm house. When I wanted quiet prayer time, I would go into one of the bathrooms to pray and read; it had become my sanctuary. One afternoon after lunch, I was walking from the lunch hall back to my building when one of the residents I did not know personally told me. "God said to stay in that mirror," I responded okay, I will. My heart became full of joy because when I was in my sanctuary, the bathroom, I always looked into the mirror when I prayed. I took this as another sign that God was with me, and His spirit was leading me.

Three months after I arrived, I received a message from my attorney that the Auburn police commission offered me twenty-five thousand dollars for pain and suffering. My attorney encouraged me to accept the offer. He explained that civil suits could go on for up to ten years due to all the appeals. I accepted the offer; it would be thirty days before I received the money. Now I had to start thinking about what I would do after receiving the money. I would not be able to stay at the shelter because my bank account would exceed what was allowed to reside there. This older lady I knew from past church experiences told me about a discipleship ministry in Texas, which housed people who struggled with addiction. The ministry's founder was from Seattle and in long-term recovery with a passion for helping others. The ministry had a men's house and a women's house. The lady I knew thought it would be good for me to volunteer and be mentored by this ministry's founder. I was excited; arrangements were made that I would come down as a volunteer and live in the women's house.

A few weeks later, I received my settlement and flew out to Texas the following week. I cleared sixteen thousand after attorney fees. I left the bulk of my cash with my mother taking five thousand dollars with me. I also packed most of my belongings because I thought I would commit one year to this ministry. Once I arrived instantly, I found out it was not what I expected. The same day I got there; I spent some time with the owner. During our visit, she told me that she would like to keep my phone for thirty days so I could experience what the other clients experience when they come to the ministry. I said OKAY without hesitation, because I was excited and thought this is where God wants me to be to grow in ministry. The house had four women, well, five including me. We all had our own rooms, which was nice. We had to be up every morning at five in the morning to go to the church for morning prayer. Once we were back home, we prepared breakfast together; after breakfast, we would have bible study. Throughout the day, we would read our Bibles, have lunch, rest time, and then prepare dinner. A few nights during the week, we would go to night service. We had good meals.

I believe most food was donated from different harvest places that sponsored the ministry. When it came to going to the store for personal needs, the director would transport us. After about three weeks, I began to need more personal time. I was becoming frustrated because one of the ladies had a puppy that would poop under my bed, and I would not know it until it was time for me to get in bed, and the smell gave it away. I felt as though living here full-time was interfering with my personal time with God. I also noticed that the one girl that was like the house mother began treating me as if I were in the program. Then I realized I was not volunteering at all. I was inducted into the discipleship ministry without my consent; it felt like it was all a trick from the beginning when she asked for my phone.

I had enough of not being able to go for a walk by myself, call my family, or watch television. I asked the house manager if she would call the director for me because I needed to talk to her. She got the director on the phone, and I told her that this was not working for me and that I wanted to get my own place, a part-time job, and volunteer at her program part-time. The director showed up shortly to talk about it with me. I explained again that living here full-time without a personal life was not what I expected when I flew all the way to Texas. The director attempted to change my mind; when I did not change my mind, the director told me to pack my bags and get out like right now. I was devastated, I thought she would give me time to find a place, but no, she treated me as though I did something wrong, like breaking one of her rules. She had me pack my bags; then, she put me out with nowhere to go. I left all my belongings on her porch and searched for a phone because she would not allow me to use hers. I walked down the street, afraid and in tears. After walking about one mile, I found a little corner store. The owner called me a cab; the first stop was back to the house to pick up my belongings from the house. Me and my belongings were in the back of this cab with no idea where I was going next. I asked the cab driver to please take me to a hotel in a non-drug area. I rented a room in a nice area and stayed there for about a week, trying to decide if I should stay or go back home. The day after I was put out of the ministry, I caught a cab to church the following evening. Once I was there, the director must have instructed the ladies in her ministry not to talk to me. The director and residents gave me the cold shoulder. I never did blame the residents because, but I was so offended and confused by the way the director continued to treat me. I thought a discipleship ministry was supposed to teach their students to walk in love as Jesus walked. I am grateful that I did not allow that experience to turn me away from the church.

CHAPTER 22

My Third Psychosis

*T*he following day, I called my mom, who was holding my cash. I explained to her what had happened, and I had chosen to stay in Texas and find someone looking for a roommate. My mom agreed that it would be good for me to stay in Texas, away from the familiar surroundings that could potentially trigger me to fall back into smoking crack. A week later, I found a girl on Craigslist looking for a roommate. She, too, was from out of state. Next, I bought a car from an older lady that posted the car for sale on craigslist. I spent the next two weeks getting familiar with my surroundings. I planned to begin looking for a church and employment in the area. One evening I was sitting on the porch reading when I noticed the neighbor next store walking back and forth to an apartment across the street. At first, I did not give much thought to it until about an hour later, I noticed him looking out his blinds every few minutes. The look he had in his eyes was a familiar look of paranoia. I decided it was time for me to go in the house because I had five months clean from crack and wanted it to stay that way. A few days later, I saw him again. This time he speaks and makes small talk before heading across the street. When he returned, he was in a hurry and did not waste his time making small talk. Just like the day before, he began peeking out his shades, looking like he was paranoid that someone or something was coming. I was triggered this time, but I did not give in; instead, I went into the house and read my Bible, prayed for strength, and called it a night. The next day, I got up early, went for a walk, stopped at a coffee shop, and planned to fill out applications at several businesses I had passed along the way. I got back to the apartment, showered, and prepared to leave when I saw that man again heading across the street. Instead of going inside and praying, I called his name and asked him if he knew where I could get some crack. He said yes, I am heading that way now. I gave him some cash, and he brought back the drugs. I did not have a pipe, so he invited me into his place to smoke. For the next few weeks, this guy (the neighbor) and I smoked drugs together until one day he was not around, so I walked to that apartment myself and bought my own crack. My roommate worked at night, so I would smoke in my room while she was at work. During the day, while she was sleeping, I would go to the neighbors and smoke. Crack had become the head of my life once again. I stopped reading my Bible; I barely prayed. I was in a dark place in a strange city where I knew no one except some random man who was getting free highs for allowing me to sit at his place and smoke. The car I bought stopped running two weeks after I bought it, so it was thrown away for two thousand dollars. Basically, I wasted away the money that was awarded to me for my pain and suffering over my husband's death.

I had decided it was time to buy a plane ticket and return home. I only had about a thousand dollars left out of the settlement. It was the last day of the month, so I told my roommate that I was planning to go back to Washington so she could start looking for a new roommate. I bought the ticket and was scheduled to leave the following day. The neighbor I had been smoking with asked his friend if he could take me to the airport and I would pay him for his time. So, I decided to get some crack and get high with the neighbor one last time before I headed back to Seattle. I remember standing in his kitchen, I took a big hit of the crack, and when I blew it out, I lost it mentally. I remember feeling intense fear, just like when I was in my apartment and heard the dogs running toward me. I experienced a blackout; I remember hearing the neighbor's voice. Once I returned to reality, I was no longer in the kitchen; I was in his living room under his coffee table. He said that I was screaming and ran and got under the coffee table. How humiliating I felt afterward; I had totally lost it in this person's home, but praise God I snapped out of it and did not end up in a psych ward in Texas, or worse, being violated by this person I hardly knew. This experience was evidence that I was in another spiritual warfare. Satan saw me in active sin, went to God, and was granted permission to torment me. Satan and his demons were having a field day in my life because I had allowed them access as soon as I bought that first piece of crack. I chose crack over God. "When an unclean spirit goes out of a man." Matthew 12:43, notice it does not say, "When the unclean spirit gets cast out of the man" Demons are not everywhere at once; they move in and out of a person. This means that the person mentioned in the Scripture was not delivered. He was relieved from a demon. At this point, a person experiences relief, not repentance. I was not delivered when I left the mission in Everett, but because my focus was on God, I was granted temporary relief. God knew that I had not wholeheartedly repented. God knew that I was holding onto unforgiveness and bitterness from my past. God knew that I had not surrendered my will to Him and that I would have another wilderness experience before I would be delivered.

Demons live in wicked, defiled, or empty places. I had become dry spiritually; I was no longer reading and praying daily. I allowed myself to become once again oppressed by the devil, experiencing the spiritual wilderness. Matthew 12:43 reads, "Goes through dry places, seeking rest, and finds none." I must admit that some demons did rest with me for a short while because I stopped pressing toward God. Yes, I was still saved and crowned by God, but God had not gotten around to cleaning me yet. There were still some things that I had to learn through this wilderness experience that God would later use for His glory.

The next morning, I missed my flight because after I tripped out, the gentleman that was going to give me a ride left the premises. Now I am stranded in a strange city with no more money and nowhere to stay. The neighbor told me about a women's domestic violence shelter. I contacted the shelter and explained that I came to volunteer in a ministry, disagreed with the director, and was put out on the streets. The shelter considered this a domestic violence matter and told be there within two hours. During my intake, I explained that I missed my flight and did not have the hundred dollars needed to change my flight. They told me to take the weekend to try and find someone from my hometown that could possibly pay the hundred dollars. I called my parents neither one would send me the hundred dollars; I called the director of the ministry and almost begged her to please pay the hundred dollars so I could get back home. My thoughts before asking her were that maybe she had some sort of remorse for how she treated me, but I was wrong; she declined to help. Monday morning, I met with one of the case managers at the shelter. She wanted my flight information. Within an hour, she came to me and said we rebooked your flight; you leave in three hours. I felt so relieved and grateful that I was headed home. This was an example of God's grace; God's grace is God giving us something we do not deserve. The Bible says, "Now to him who works, the wages are not counted as grace but as debt. But to him who does not work but believes on Him who justifies the ungodly, his faith is accounted for righteousness" (Romans 4:4-5). God's grace gave me what I did not earn or deserve. As I began to mature in Christ, I had to learn not to take advantage of God's grace by continuing with the same attitude and sinful desires. God's grace transformed me little by little every minute of the day. My oldest daughter picked me up from the airport and allowed me to stay with her once again. I stayed with her for a few weeks before deciding to call the mission in Everett to see if I could come back. They said I could come back, but I had to be there by the next day, or they would give my spot away. I called a friend of mine and asked if she could give me a ride to Everett; she agreed but asked why I would want to go back to a shelter. I told her that God had begun a work in me at that shelter, but I made the mistake of leaving there before I was equipped and confident in God. John 15:5 reads, "I am the vine; you are the branches. If you remain in me and I in you, you will bear much fruit; apart from me, you can do nothing." Jesus is teaching us that we cannot live a fruitful life, a life filled with lasting impact, without learning to be attached to God and becoming God-reliant. So, I needed to return to the mission to learn to be reliant on God because my self-reliance (my flesh) was destroying me, just as the devil had been attempting to do since I was eleven.

CHAPTER 23

Crowned With Royalty

I made it to the mission around 3 pm. I instantly felt a sense of peace when I stepped on those grounds. It felt like God was standing there waiting for me with His arms open wide, just like He did with the prodigal son. Luke 15:22 reads, "The Father quickly told one of his servants to bring out and put upon his son, who stood in rags, the best robe, ring, and sandals. "Each item contains a priceless and profound insight into the character of God's love toward all those who are His and bear the title of son or daughter. He pulled out the best robe just for me and laid it around my shoulders. God was not looking at my disobedience; He was looking at me as the one lost sheep that was finally found. The day I arrived at the mission was the last day I desired to use drugs. God totally delivered me from addiction that day. God knew I could not bear to continue living the rollercoaster ride of addiction, so he said today is your day for freedom. I was able to say goodbye to crack the one thing I allowed to be the head of my life for years.

"Dear Crack, when we first met, we became lovers. I fell in love with you so quickly. We could stay up all night and just hang out every weekend. Then I began looking forward to seeing you every day. Then I had to start searching for you and our relationship became one-sided. Our time together was no longer fun I had to see you, or I would get emotionally sick with depression and suicidal thoughts. You slowly took important parts of my life from me: my family, my friends, my job, my home, all my money, and my freedom. But most of all, you took away my self-worth and my inner beauty. You left me with nothing except an addiction that was slowly destroying me spiritually, and you did not care. You even tried to take my life. I knew then that our affair had to end. I now know you never wanted the best for me. You just wanted to destroy my self-worth. A real lover looks out for your best interest and really cares. They do not strip you of everything positive and make you want to die; they root for you to live to become your best person. I have to say goodbye for good because you are not good for me, and I hope I can share my story and warn others about you before it is too late for them to build a meaningful life serving God. With God's love and guidance, I can say goodbye crack addition; you no longer have the power to control my life. I have found my freedom in God who loves me and who sees me as royalty."

CHAPTER 24

God Transformed
My Life

My first week back at the mission, I attended the morning and evening devotions. I could not read my bible because I had lost my glasses. Sunday came around, so I went to church with a couple of the ladies that were also living at the mission. This was my first-time attending church in months, and God met me there. I was unable to follow along with reading the scripture due to not having my glasses. The service was impressive. The presence of God was in that place; people were praising with their hands lifted to God. On the bus ride home, I felt the presence of God all over me. I heard Him speak to my spirit. He told me to write a letter to three local optometrists and tell them about my living situation. When I got back to my room, I wrote the letters; I explained I was homeless and needed to find employment, but I could not fill out applications because

I needed glasses. I ended the letter by writing if they could bless me with a pair of glasses, God would bless them in return. I prayed over the letters and mailed them. Within a week, I received a phone call from the office manager of one of the optometrists. She said that they would like to schedule an appointment for me to come in for an exam. I hung up that phone and just cried and thanked God. God said to me it was your faith that paved the way. Within ten days, I had my new glasses and began going to temp agencies in hopes of finding employment. Two days later, I was given a long-term assignment at stockpot. They are a soup company in Everett that makes all the soups sold in Fred-Meyers and Safeway grocery stores. I worked for two months before getting hired as a permanent employee. By now, I had been at the mission for three months. Since I was employed, I was accepted into the transitional program in another building. In this program, I had a roommate who was working as well. For the next few months, I continued to attend morning devotions, I worked hard, saved all my money, and bought a car. Now I was able to go to Church on Sunday mornings; the issue was that I was in Everett where there were few Black churches. See, all I knew was Pentecostals or Church of God and Christ, predominantly Black denominations. I decided to step out of the familiar and attend a non-denomination Christian church. I stepped into this church and was overwhelmed by the presence of God. The church service had not started yet, but the worship team was worshipping like there was a room full of people. This was an awakening; this day is when I realized God's presence is everywhere. I realized that it is not the drums playing or the piano playing that usher in the presence of God. It is about spending time with God daily and yielding to the Holy Spirit within us ushers us into His presence, so when we arrive at an anointed building, we are overwhelmed by His presence. James 4:8–"Draw near to God, and He will draw near to you. Cleanse your hands, you sinners; and purify your hearts, you double-minded."

Psalms 27:8–"When You said, "Seek My face," my heart said to You, "Your face, Lord, I will seek." On a rare occasion, I would drive to Auburn to visit my mother and daughters. I remember driving down certain blocks when I would hear the Holy Spirit say to me "don't go down that block." God was leading my steps and keeping me out of harm's way as I visited my family. The blocks He instructed me not to go down were blocks where Satan was waiting to tempt me to go back to what God delivered me from. To this day, fifteen years later, I still hear God say beware as I go down those blocks in Auburn, Wash. This shows me that Satan is still waiting to catch me slipping so he can tempt me to sin and lose my deliverance. Satan is known for being a great tempter. If I did not obey God and went down the wrong block, he could have possibly tempted me to stop by an old drug dealer's house to see how they were doing. Luke 22:31. Jesus says,

"Simon, Simon, behold, Satan demanded to have you, that he might sift you like wheat."

Once I arrived at my mother's house, I felt like a stranger; I was uncomfortable around my family. Today I know it was because I was becoming more like God, and my desires were God's desires. I no longer had things in common with my family because they were the same, but I was changing. I can see my family is still divided in many ways still to this day. Luke 12:52-53 reads; For from now on in one house there will be five divided, three against two and two against three. They will be divided, father against son and son against father, mother against daughter and daughter against mother, mother-in-law against her daughter-in-law, and daughter-in-law against mother-in-law." Praying for God to heal toxic behaviors, feelings of neglect, or conflict that have caused feelings of animosity in my immediate family.

Nine months had passed, and I was selected to move from the mission into a house owned by the mission; the house was in a quiet neighborhood, it had six bedrooms and three bathrooms, and the rent was only $400 a month. All my housemates were Christians working and doing their own thing. I still worked graveyard, so my routine was simple. I woke up at 7 pm, showered, had a light dinner, and then studied and prayed for an hour before heading off to work. Every night I would stop at the Seven-Eleven on the corner for coffee and a doughnut. I was still smoking cigarettes during this time, so I would drink my coffee and smoke a cigarette with the cashier. I talked about the desire God had placed on my heart to be a Chaplain, so it was time for me to pray for God to deliver me from the habit of smoking cigarettes. In the same week, I received a call from a bishop I had been acquainted with through a friend. He said to me that God instructed him to ordain me as a minister of the Gospel. I was shocked; I did not feel as though that was my calling, but he insisted it was the will of God. The next Saturday, I went to his home for a private ceremony with the bishop, his wife, and my acquaintance that had introduced us two years prior. When I got back home, I put the ordination certificate in my dresser drawer. Two days later, I showed up as always at the seven-eleven for my coffee and doughnut. The cashier was so excited to see me, that she shared that earlier that day, two chaplains came into the store, and she told them she had a friend who was interested in learning more about Chaplaincy, and one of the Chaplains left her with instructions for me to give her a call. I called the number, talked with the Chaplain, and explained to her the encounter I had with a chaplain when I was in deep in crisis and how I wanted to be that person for someone in a crisis. The Chaplain explained the process and the name of the organization that comes to WA twice a year for a 48-hour chaplaincy training. The organization was called the International Fellowship of Chaplains. I was instructed to go to their website and apply for the training.

One of the requirements to be considered for the training was I had to be an ordained minister of the Gospel. When I read that requirement, I burst into tears because I had just been ordained two weeks prior. God had set it up; he knew for me to be considered for this training; I would need to be ordained. This was when I began to understand what it meant to have God open doors that no man could shut. Ephesians 1:11-12 reads," In him we were also chosen, having been predestined according to the plan of him who works out everything in conformity with the purpose of his will, in order that we … might be for the praise of his glory." This is proof that God engages in our daily lives to accomplish His purpose and equips and opens doors to ensure it is accomplished in His perfect timing, even if we feel we are not ready for the call. Four weeks later, I took my forty-eight hours of vacation and attended certification training. On the final day of the training, we had an hour to complete the final exam. When the hour was up, I had not finished all the questions. One of the volunteers took my exam to the head Chaplain during the training and explained that I had not completed the exam. The Chaplain called me to his desk, looked at me, and said I have been watching you all week, and I want you to know you have the pure heart of a chaplain. He took my unfinished exam, placed it on the bottom of his pile, and said you will get something in the mail in a few weeks. When the mail arrived, I opened it and inside was my badge and my certificate.

The letter with the certificate said congratulations because of your references and prior ordination; you are ordained as a Chaplain. Tears rolled again because God took a girl with no ministry experience and ordained her by a well-known bishop, opening the door for me to be ordained as a Chaplain. BUT GOD, WON'T HE DO IT!!

CHAPTER 25

Ministry Birthed

One Sunday, I decided to visit a Church in downtown Seattle. While I was walking near the courthouse where the unhoused slept, a man came up to me and asked if he could walk with me; since we were in the open, I replied sure. He said he wanted to share with me how to reach the lost people who were homeless. He began by saying good morning, the first time you walk through the park. The next time you walk through the same park, ask the same individual their name. The next time you walk through the park, that same individual will see you coming and put away their drugs, and you say hello using their name. The next time the same individual sees you, they will say, "Here comes my friend. After the man was finished sharing, he walked away down the street saying, "have a good day." I was puzzled as to why he would share this information with me. The next week I received a call from a sister in Christ; she said I have a name for your ministry. The Love Connection, I said, what ministry. She responded the ministry God is birthing in you. I had no idea what kind of ministry God was birthing in me, but I believed this lady had a revelation from God, so I applied for a non-profit license with the State of Washington. A few weeks later, one of my young co-workers found out that I was a Chaplain. He came to me saying he needed to complete twenty hours of community and asked if I could help him out. I had just received my non-profit, so I said yes, but had no idea what type of community service work he and I could do together. It was November of 2008 and cold outside, so I said we could pass out hats and gloves to the homeless living in downtown Seattle. He and I asked all our co-workers to donate twenty dollars to the cause. The next week we had enough cash to purchase fifty pairs of hats and gloves. We went downtown and passed those out and were asked did we have any socks. The following week we went downtown and passed out socks and gloves. This was the birth of The Love Connection Homeless Outreach Ministry. We served the homeless as the gentleman who walked with me instructed. For the next two years, I continued living and working in Everett, and my ministry began to grow. In the Winter of 2009, my employer allowed me to have a coat drive at the facility. I put two big boxes around the facility, The coat drive went on for three weeks, and I ended up with ten big black garbage bags of coats and a total of six hundred dollars donated. Ten co-workers volunteered to come and hand out the supplies. To this day, Stockpot in Everett has annual coat drives. In January of 2010, I began volunteering at the Women's Mission once a week, facilitating the morning devotion. This was the first of many instances where God sent me back to where I started to be a blessing to others by sharing the courage, strength, and hope I have gained by serving Christ. During this time, I had thoughts of going to seminary college, but God said no; He said I want to be your teacher. I believe God did not want me to get caught up in religious views; He wanted the Holy Spirit to be the one to teach and guide me into all truth.

CHAPTER 26

Boldness In Christ

One afternoon, I was catching the bus to meet two of my daughters in downtown Seattle for lunch. While riding the bus, this gentleman gets on the front, plops down, and says, "I am done." The gentleman sitting across from him said, "man, just give it a break for a while." This man said again loudly, "I am done." I remember sitting straight up and saying, excuse me, sir, are you saying you are done with the way you are living? He responded, yes, someone gets it. I then asked him if he would like me to pray for him? To my surprise, he said yes. I remember feeling nervous because I had never prayed for someone spontaneously before. I went to him, took his hands, and prayed for him. The gentleman across from him started saying, " No one has ever prayed for me, I went over to him, and again he said, "No one has ever prayed for me." This Holy Ghost's boldness was all over me; I told him, if you be quiet, I will pray for you. After praying for them, I went back to my seat, still standing up. On the left side of me was an older Black man; he said someone does what they're supposed to do about time. On my right side was a Caucasian man; he said we are in this together, sister. On the set to my right was a nun just looking at me with the love of God. Finally, we stopped, and the man on my right walked off the bus and just disappeared into thin air. Then it hit me I was entertaining my guardian angels. God evaluated me to see if I could manage the call to outreach ministry. I had all the personal skills needed, including being friendly, empathetic, a good listener, an analytical person, enthusiastic, gentle, persistent, flexible, ethical, trustworthy, and the most important skill, a passion for sharing the gospel of Jesus Christ.

One Sunday, I went to Church service in downtown Seattle, it was held in the Fry hotel. Individuals occupied the hotel with active addiction or mental health issues. The church service consisted mostly of residents of the hotel. The loud music and brewing coffee smell encouraged the residents to check out the service. There was this lady in the service with her young son. The Pastor came over to me and told me to go and pray for the lady. I said no, I cannot; he said yes, you can, so do it now. He said it with such authority in his voice that I walked over to the lady and asked if she wanted prayer. She instantly stood up and lifted her hand in the air. As I began to pray for the lady, the Holy Spirit led me to touch her from head to toe to those watching; it most likely looked like I was frisking her looking for her drugs. When I got to her feet, she jumped up, shouting I am free, I am free. Instantly I heard the spirit of God say to me shake it off. So, I began walking around the church praying in the spirit, shaking my hands. It looked like I was shaking my hands dry. The lady ran out of the room up to her apartment, came back down, and through her drug pipes in the middle of the church floor. She began testifying. She said, "when you touched my feet, I felt free; it felt like God yanked that spirit of addiction right out of my body." The church began praising God by singing and dancing in the spirit. I am not sure what happened to that lady; I have no idea if she stayed clean, but I do know that when we are obedient and pray, miracles still happen today.

A few weeks later, I went downtown to the same church service. Once I arrived, I saw an ambulance out front, then I saw the paramedics walk out a lady that had attended the service the last time I was there. I asked the lady if she was okay. She said no, you know those voices keep coming back. As she was entering the ambulance, I told her I would be praying for her. Once I was inside, the Pastor told me that she had schizophrenia and had recently reported to her that she had been doing better and decided to stop taking her prescribed medications. Maybe an hour later, I saw the lady walking past the church door; I did not think much of it then and kept enjoying the service. Fifteen minutes later, the owner of the restaurant next door runs into the church, yelling that a woman was lying on the cement in the alley. To our surprise, it was the lady who walked by our church door. She must have been walking to the elevator to take her to the tenth floor where she resided. That poor lady was under distress in a real crisis that led her to commit suicide that day. If I knew about mental illness then, as I do today, I would have road with her to the hospital to be sure she got the help she needed. Mental illness is real, addiction is real, and the devil is real. Today I understand that people with mental illness need spiritual and physical help.

CHAPTER 27

God Said No, I Said Yes

*I*n May of 2009, one of my male co-workers saw that I did not have a CD player in my car, so he surprised me with one for my birthday. He then asked me out to dinner, and we began dating. From the beginning, I was not physically attracted to him but to his attention and kindness. He was respectful of my decision to live a celibate lifestyle unless I was married. We dated for six months, and then he asked me to marry him, and I said yes. We planned the wedding; I purchased the lavender dresses for my four daughters. His sister was flying in from Atlanta, Georgia; everything was set. Three weeks before the wedding, I felt in my heart that I was not supposed to marry this man. I talked to my good friend, a strong Christian, about my second thoughts. She said those feelings were normal, reassuring me that everything would be just fine. So, I went with what she said and buried my own unction that was strong in my spirit. One week before the wedding, I had the feeling of doubt again, but this time

I did not share them with anyone. I told myself I could not cancel the wedding his sister bought her plane ticket. Now it was our wedding day; I was so anxious but went through with it despite knowing in my heart it was not the plans God had for me. The officiant over our wedding was the same Bishop that had ordained me. After we said our vows and signed the paperwork, the Bishop asked me if I wanted to file it myself, and I said yes. I am an officiant today, and I know the rules are the officiant over the wedding is responsible for making sure the paperwork is filed to make the union legal.

Now we are married; we had moved into a nice one-bedroom apartment one week before our wedding. We enjoyed our honeymoon just like any other newlywed couple. We both still worked for the same company but on different shifts, so there was not a lot of intimacy going on, but there was some. We had four weeks to submit the paperwork, or the union would not be valid. One week before the deadline, I had just gotten home from work, and I talked to my prayer partner as I did every morning. I was looking for something on my dresser and saw the marriage license application. I picked it up and said to my prayer partner; I do not believe God wants me to file this paperwork because I was not supposed to marry him in the first place. Before filing this paperwork, I decided to pray and seek God for the answer. When I got to work that night, I saw my guy, he said to me Tammie, why don't you put the paperwork on the table, and I will file it in the morning. I remember bursting into tears and telling him I did not believe I was supposed to be married to him. We agreed to talk about it when I got home from work. The next morning, I explained to him the doubts I had before our wedding day and the same doubts I had at that moment. I told him that I was praying to be certain. He was tearful and did not say much. Two days later, I tore the paperwork up because this marriage was a mistake and would interfere with me continuing to find my purpose in God. I also told him that I had repented to God because I felt I had fornicated because my heart was never union focused. I told him that I could no longer sleep with him but would stay in the apartment until the lease was up in four months he agreed.

Three weeks before my lease was up, I got a call that my mother had been taken to the emergency because she had woken up coughing up blood. I rushed to the hospital the next morning after work. My mother said the bleeding was caused by scar tissue on her lungs from the radiation she had five years ago when she had lung cancer. But that was not the truth. Her lung cancer had come out of remission, but she did not want us to worry that she was in stage four cancer, and there was nothing they could do. I decided it was time to move back closer to my family. By this time, it had been three years since I was delivered from crack cocaine, and I was strong in my walk with God. The week before I was supposed to move, my guy had not been to the apartment for more than a day, and I was concerned about him. Finally, he showed up, and I was relieved that he was okay. Although I knew he was not the man for me, he was a special friend of mine, and I wanted the best for him. He confessed to me that he had been out gambling and had spent his entire paycheck, including rent money. Right then, in my heart, I began praising Jesus for showing me before it was too late that this man still struggled with addictions, and that was not the life he planned for me. God delivered me from a life of chaos. No way would he send me a mate with those same struggles. I learned from this experience to never second guess the warnings you feel in your spirit. Jeremiah 25:7 reads, "But you would not listen to me," says the Lord. "You made me furious by worshiping idols you made with your own hands, bringing on yourselves all the disasters you now suffer."

CHAPTER 28

Walking In Forgiveness

*T*he week before I was set to move back to Kent, I received a call from my oldest daughter. While I was on the phone with her, I heard moaning in the background. I asked my daughter what that sound was, and she told me it was her father, who was dying from stomach cancer. At that moment, I was no longer his victim; I was a child of God full of empathy and mercy for this man who had raped me for years. Tears welled up in my eyes, and I prayed for him; I asked God to forgive him and relieve his suffering. He passed away later that night. I cannot say he made it into heaven because I do not believe in his sick mind; he felt he had done anything wrong. Although we in our right minds know sexual abuse is morally wrong, many offenders create and reinforce 'thinking errors' to rationalize and minimize the impact of their abuse. I believe since he took his time with me and did not physically harm me, that I would not be damaged. And he was right; I was not damaged; I was just emotionally sick for a long time but praised God for Jesus who died to set the captives free. That day I was free to forgive him, freed from the root of bitterness, freed from using drugs to self-medicate. From that day forward, I was able to share my story without feeling any guilt or shame for someone else's sin. That day was the beginning of my inner healing. No more chains were holding me from walking in my purpose.

Since I was quitting my job to relocate, I was eligible for unemployment. The plan was that I would stay with my father and enroll in school. I was with my father for about two weeks before he gave me one week to find another place to stay. All because while I was on hold with unemployment, a call rang in on the other line, and I did not answer it because it was important for me to get my call through. When I was finished with the call, he was upset about missing his phone call that he asked me to leave. I was devastated because he and I had planned this move three months prior, and I had quit my job expecting his support. He must have felt guilty because he left me a check for twelve hundred dollars on my bed the following day.

I went and stayed with my oldest daughter for about six months. I was receiving my unemployment, so I focused on doing outreach ministry. I had coat drives and used my finances to purchase hygiene supplies and socks for homeless people. I felt awkward being around my family because they were all grown up living their own lives, and

I did not know them anymore. I had spent the last three years healing from my past, and in the years prior, I was in active addiction. I missed a lot and knew I could not get those years back, so I had to focus on the present. During this time, I realized that my oldest daughter did not have a lot of respect for me. Sometimes she would go days without really talking to me, and we were living in the same house. At that time of my journey, I deserved the treatment and hoped we would become closer in time. It is now twelve years later with some change. Recently she stated, "I grew up as a teenager and young adult with hurt, anger, and disappointments. I had to grow up a lot faster than other kids my age. Part of me is thankful because that forced me to become strong and independent. I have been able to let go of some of the hurt and am glad you are still here, and we are able to have a relationship. It may not be the type of mother-daughter relationship I envisioned, but I have had to accept that it is what it is." As I am writing this today, I also must accept that "it is what it is." For me, this hurt because I do not feel we have a healthy relationship because of the lack of respect that she has for me due to my mistakes as a person and as a mother. Honestly, if I were in any one of my daughters' shoes, I would be angry. As I wrote at the beginning of this memoir, I missed major events in their lives, and they have the right to their feelings and perspective toward me. Today I was tearful writing this because I have learned in recovery that we must accept the things we cannot change.

My past I cannot change, and their right to their feelings I cannot change. But one thing I don't do anymore, is beat myself up over my past. I have almost sixteen years clean; I have asked for forgiveness for past events; as I said earlier, I do not have the power to change anything that has already occurred. I must continue to move forward from this point on by realizing that my adult children must find their way to heal.

CHAPTER 29

They Both Got Their Wings

*O*ne afternoon, I received a call from my second oldest daughter telling me that my mother had passed out on the street close to her home and was airlifted to Harborview Hospital. I rushed to the hospital, and when I arrived, I saw my brother sitting in a waiting room. He informs me that our mother had a cardiac arrest after getting off the bus, and one of her neighbors saw her lying on the sidewalk. When we were able to go back and see her, I could tell she was not going to walk out alive. I smelled death, and she was hooked up to all these machines. She was in ICU. We were encouraged to go home and come back in the morning. Once we arrived, we had a family meeting with the Doctors, and they informed us that she had been unconscious for twenty minutes and there would likely be brain damage if she did wake up. They also informed us that her cancer had returned and was in the late stages.

My brother and I decided to take her off the ventilator because she would want it that way. We were all in the room, including my aunt and cousins who had driven all night from Idaho" to say our last goodbyes. The nurse slowly began lowering the Oxygen. Suddenly, I heard one of my daughters yells, "she is turning blue." Suddenly, I yell at the nurses wait, I must pray. I remember lying over my mom asking God to have mercy on her soul for me. Then I hear my daughter say, "she's crying." Tears rolled down her cheeks; she then moved her head back and forth and was pronounced dead. In my heart of hearts, I believe God heard my cry and had mercy on her soul. I say this because my mom did not attend church, and I had never seen her open a bible in all my years. Three months later, my father passed away from cancer. I was blessed to officiate both of my parents' funerals. Although they were alive, they carried the burden of worrying about me and taking care of my daughters; I felt so blessed that I was sober and in a sound mind before they both went on to Glory. If you remember reading earlier, I had prayed and asked God not to allow my mother to die while I was still in addiction. God honored that prayer. Today I have regrets about not getting closer to my mother once I was freed from drugs. I also fear that my daughters are going to have the same regrets when I pass away.

CHAPTER 30

The Latter Will Be Greater

*T*he last ten years of my life have been full of accomplishments. I was invited to Lagos, Nigeria, as an American Speaker for a Chaplaincy Conference in two thousand thirteen. I was elated; I found two people that were interested in traveling with me until the last minute they both declined. I had worked hard to get sponsors, so I bought my ticket and went to Africa alone. I had chaperones waiting for me at the airport and once I arrived in Africa. In Africa, I preached the Gospel four days out of the nine I was there. I visited many homes in a rural area of Lagos and experienced the culture. On my last evening there, the ladies of the village insisted on pampering me by doing my nails outside on the porch. Within days after returning home, I began feeling exhausted and had a high fever. I went to urgent care with a temperature of one hundred and four; yes, I had Malaria, and it took two months for me to recover.

In two thousand fifteen, I went back to college at the age of fifty. I graduated two thousand eighteen with a degree specializing in substance use disorders. My first employment as a substance use disorder specialist was at Residence Twelve, the last inpatient treatment center I spent twenty-eight days attempting to handle my addiction.

In two thousand eighteen, the next place God sent me back to as a substance use disorder professional was the Women's Corrections Facility, the same facility that I did time at back in nineteen ninety-one. This is where I got the idea to write a book. Initially, the vision was to get six women with similar stories to mine to write their stories. The book's purpose was to show society that women do not just wake up one day and say hello, world; I am going to smoke crack and waste away in prison. These women in prison were the victim of circumstances just like I was, and they had a story to tell. Before I could start the project with the ladies, I got a call from the Department of Corrections. They heard about my vision project and wanted to interrogate me about it. The prison thought the project was about corruption in the system. So, I thought it best that I put the project on hold. A few months later, I heard God say draft your story. The readers need to see God's glory and know that abuse, addiction, or incarceration does not have to define their futures.

Currently, I am employed as a Clinical Supervisor for Recovery Place Kent. This facility is on the same property as the detox I went to back in the day when the attendant washed my feet. I remember when he said to me, "Jesus washed all his disciples' feet." I am sharing this memoir, my story, the good and the bad, the positive and the negative, to show you that God uses us through our suffering, and our testimonies empower others that they too can make it out of their sufferings. Being a Christian clinician is overwhelming spiritually at times because the patients that come in who are Christian are not fully heard. When the patients talk about hearing from God and seeing the darkness in the building is labeled as just being delusional and are not really being heard. Providers tend to stand on the belief that when individuals say they hear God or they talk to God, it is a delusion; this comes from the teaching of Sigmund Freud. "Sigmund Freud considered believing in a single god to be a delusion. He also stated that religion "comprises a system of wishful illusions together with a disavowal of reality, such as we find in an isolated from nowhere else but amentia, in a state of blissful hallucinatory confusion." From my personal experience with mental health issues, while using substances, I could not have survived without my belief in God. I have learned personally and professionally that religion and spirituality can positively impact mental health.

Today my relationships with my daughters are not always the best; I have faith that one day they will decide to commit their lives to Christ where they will find the freedom to forgive. They are the image of myself before

I surrendered to Christ. I was not able to heal and forgive. But through Christ, I was able to do what I never thought was possible: to forgive my mother and the man who took away my innocence. God transformed my heart to resemble His. God took my past suffering and turned it into a testimony that gives others hope. Today I am still enduring some grief, but nothing I cannot manage with God leading my steps.

God Brings Us Suffering For The Sake Of Others

*I*n 2 Corinthians, Paul says that he wants many to join in praying for him so that, as God sustains him, God will get more glory. Paul knows sharing suffering and bearing each other's burdens gives God glory. It is humbling to let people in on our weaknesses, but it serves to highlight God's powerful sustaining grace. Ongoing pain and suffering tend to isolate us from one another. We get sick of being "the sick one" and tired of being "the one who is always worn out." We do not like revealing our weaknesses. But God receives glory when we let others in to see his strength in our weakness. God receives glory when we do not act like we have it all together but instead admit that God is holding us together through the gospel of his Son, the ministry of his Spirit, and the prayers of his people. We are fellow heirs with Jesus Christ, sons, and daughters of the living God. And because of this relationship, the all-powerful Ruler of the universe is also a Father of mercies and a God of all comfort. Roman 8: 13-17 Here, Paul says that God comforts them in all their afflictions. There is no affliction that God is unaware of or distant from. God is infinitely interested in the care and comfort of his children in all their afflictions. So, we are never alone in our suffering, whatever the pain or loss might be. As we look to God for comfort and hope in suffering, he means to impart in us the heart to comfort others who are being afflicted with the same comfort we have received from God. God comforted me so I can comfort you and many others before you. God granted me mercy so that I could be merciful to others. God stood with me through my years of suffering, so I will stand whole-heartedly with others suffering. God never leaves me alone in my suffering, so I will not leave others alone in theirs. God means we should not let our suffering become an excuse to keep our weakness hidden or to just focus on ourselves. We must be ready to share our comfort during suffering because God's glory is at stake and because the sufferers are many.

(https://www.desiringgod.org/articles/
god-brings-us-suffering-for-others-sake)

CHAPTER 32

Helping A Sister Through Her Pain

*I*n two thousand and nineteen, I was honored to donate my left kidney to a sister suffering from kidney failure. I decided to share an article that explains the details.

"Love in Action: A 'golden ticket' that saved this woman's life."

As the story goes, Analisa Mitchell, at that time, 46 years old and wearily clinging to life, barely made it to the WOW retreat, and Tammie Holmes, then fifty-five, a self-described introvert out of her comfort zone attending, did it anyway. While the ladies were receiving room assignments and settling in, Holmes, not ready to face the crowd, recalls starting a conversation with Mitchell, who sat near the fireplace, not looking well. "Tammie turned her attention toward me," Mitchell recalls. This fateful meeting and the conversation that followed would bind these women together in a way neither could have imagined. Holmes would learn of Mitchell's history with Lupus, her then-recent month-long hospital stay, and the critical impact of the disease on Mitchell's kidneys. "I told Tammie how I had just been discharged from the hospital, that I almost passed away," says Mitchell, still determined as she was to be there at the retreat and living this life. She explained that she was pressed to get well quickly — well enough to be considered a candidate for a kidney transplant. But for as long as Mitchell had been hoping to gain strength to withstand a transplant, she had also been waiting for a kidney that would be a match. In that time, she had become sensitized, meaning her antibody levels had become exceptionally elevated, more than certain to fight against a donor's kidney. The human body in a "sensitized" state can reject even a matching donor organ. Safeguarding against this and other concerns had prolonged Mitchell's wait. "At that time, I had been waiting for more than eight years," she says. This devastating bottom line was compounding the difficulty presented by Mitchell's sensitized state: only 2% of the living donor population could save her life. Ninety-eight percent, she already knew, were incompatible. Hearing this, Holmes remembered a story of a woman who became her aunt's kidney donor, and she retold that story to Mitchell, adding, "I was so moved that I told God, if I had the opportunity, I would [do the same]. God planted the seed that day." And Holmes says, "without hesitation, I told Analisa that I came to the retreat just for her and that I would give her a kidney." Mitchell says it was like "the opportunity presented itself [to Holmes], and she stepped out." Before the end of the retreat, the two had traded contact information and become Facebook friends. Holmes would often share her research about kidney donation and all it entails. "She would tell me what I learned and what I needed to do," Mitchell recalls. Finally, after a year, she was healthy enough to undergo surgery. But, in January 2019, after a battery of tests, after quickly dropping twenty pounds over four months on doctor's orders, after countless blood draws, and more, Holmes says, "I found out I wasn't a perfect match for Analisa." It had been a long and sometimes incredibly disappointing process for both women. Nevertheless, for Holmes, having come to this exceptional place of sacrifice, fearlessness, peace of mind, and intention, there was simply no way she was turning back now. It would not all be in vain. When her kidney was found to be incompatible with Mitchell, she chose to present her offer to the National Kidney Registry, where a match was determined in two days. Holmes' kidney would be a gift to a father and his family in Baltimore. Following surgery in July, was a month of rest at home. Some residual fatigue and water retention are her only complaints. But it was by this turn of events that Holmes received what is called a voucher. It is the golden ticket in the world of organ donation. A candidate for a kidney transplant who holds a voucher, or is named as the beneficiary of a voucher, is prioritized on the National Kidney Registry. Holmes named Mitchell as a beneficiary of that voucher. Just two weeks later, Mitchell received the long-awaited call from The Registry, followed by her kidney transplantation in September. They have no regret about all they have been through. If they, had it to do again, they would. "Absolutely," says Mitchell. "It's the most humane thing I've ever done," says Holmes. "I would do it again in a heartbeat." ("Afroliterati® (Carla Bell) – Medium») written by «Carla Bell»

My kidney was transported to Virginia by a man that was a husband and father. In the summer of two-thousand-twenty-one, I took a road trip to Virginia and met the man who was blessed with my left kidney. All I can say is that it was the best feeling I had ever had. The room was filled with gratitude and unconditional love. My heart tells me that if I never do anything else, I have done enough. I gave the gift of life, and two individuals can now enjoy their lives with their families. People will ask me why I would do it for a stranger. My answer is always why not. You see, I was at a church service twenty years prior, and a lady there shared her testimony about donating a kidney to her aunt. I remember saying if I ever had the opportunity to do that, I would. I believe God had prepared my heart that day in that church service to be a living organ donor. God gets all the glory and praise. I was just being obedient to the call of service.

QUESTIONS AND ANSWERS

I am going to end this memoir with the most asked questions that I receive when sharing my testimony on a platform.

Q. What finally motivated you to ask for help or make a change (can you describe your "moment of clarity"?

A. My mind, body, and soul had enough. I had to make the decision, did I want God, or did I want to continue living a life of spiritual torment? Every time I would use drugs, I would have instant fear. The world would say I experienced delusions, but I say I was spiritually attacked by demons and principalities in my mind, and I wanted to be free which meant I had to learn to say yes to God and no to drugs.

Q. What services in the community did you utilize to start your recovery?

A. The Everett women's gospel mission shelter was my saving grace. I lived and participated in their services for two years. Also attending Church in the community together these two resources helped me get to where I am today, free from drugs and tormenting spirits for fifteen years and counting.

Q. Have you done things under the influence of drugs that you would not have done if drugs were not a factor?

A. The only time I ever did anything illegal or immoral is when I was under the influence of drugs. I committed crimes, I lied, I stole from my family, and wrote checks that I knew were bad. I neglected my children by not being physically or emotionally there. I have had sexual relations with a few men just for their money or drugs while under the influence.

Q. If you have had previous relapses, what were some of the contributing factors?

A. I have had numerous relapses in the past. The main reason is I thought I could do it on my own by just going to church and running to the altar for prayer. I would tell myself I do not need a program I got God. God is my main source today, but it is also very important to have a support network that understands a person's struggles and weaknesses that can assist with keeping you accountable for your recovery process. Another big mistake I would make is going back to areas where I previously used drugs.

People, places, and things are triggers and it is important to know our triggers and avoid them at all costs or we will fall into relapse.

Q. What recovery path speaks most to you and why? Did you try anything before that did not work?

A. My path consisted of putting God first in my life. I meditated, read my bible, and worshipped daily. I was living in the Everett Gospel Mission which is faith-based. They had meditation and bible study morning and evening. I was surrounded by like-minded women meaning we were all in early recovery. We empowered one another daily with the word of God, prayer, and listening skills. We were a group of women who related to one another and were suffering the same consequences due to our substance use. We were each other's accountability partners cheering one another to succeed. Yes, I tried sober support meetings in the community. In the past, I had been court-ordered to attend NA sober support meetings in the community. At that time, they did nothing for me because I was not ready to receive what they had to offer. Once I became a counselor, I

would attend AA/NA meetings with clients and left empowered by the stories I heard in those rooms. I encourage my clients today to be active participants in AA or NA.

Q. How would you define spirituality in simple terms and what is your opinion of the role spirituality plays in recovery?

A. Spirituality involves the recognition of a feeling, sense, or belief that there is something greater than me that can and will restore my soul to sanity. Without my spiritual belief that there is a God, Father, Son, and Holy Spirit I would not be where I am today. My faith and trust in God who is a spiritual being is what gives me the strength needed daily to continue to walk in freedom from addiction.

Q. Some people say that addiction is a disease, and others believe it is a choice. What do you think, and why?

A. It is a disease by choice. Meaning we make the first choice to use drugs but after time we no longer have the choice. Addiction is now mentioned in the Diagnostic and Statistical Manual published by the American Psychiatric Association (DSM). With it being mentioned in this book, the idea cannot be dismissed about it being a disease (Leyton, Marco). This book is used to look up diseases and learn more about the overview, symptoms, and possible cures. All the diseases known are listed. It is like the dictionary or encyclopedia of human diseases.

Q. I assume addiction comes with regrets; What are your biggest regrets?

A. My biggest regret is the impact that my drug use has had on my family. My past mistakes somewhat effect their personal well-being and sanity; It has been almost sixteen years since God changed my life; I pray that all my daughters get the email that momma has changed and moved on. So they to can move on and leave healthy lives without regrets.

WHY I DO WHAT I DO

Dear Ms. Holmes, I am wishing you nothing but happiness on your special day. I just want to say thank you for always going beyond to help us and believing in us when we did not believe in ourselves. You are an amazing person inside and out. Thank you for everything you do. Happy Birthday Ms. Holmes.

Dearest Ms. Holmes, Happy Belated Birthday! You deserve only the best because you are really a wonderful woman. I am blessed to have met you and now have you in my life. Thank you for allowing me to open-up to you and listening to my story, without judging me. I hope I will be able to open-up to you more in the future. I look up to you a lot, because even after all you have been through in your life, you became such a strong, fierce woman that I truly idolize in my life. Sorry I could not give you a fancier card for your birthday, but I want you to know that this letter comes straight from my heart. God Bless You Ms. Holmes.

Ms. Holmes, thank you for being you! I know God put you in my life so I could see his light shining through you. Thank you for being such an excellent teacher and making it easier to absorb what you were putting out. I know many times you did not even have to speak words and I still felt God's presence through you. Thank you for being transparent and sharing your story with me. I will always remember you.

Dear Ms. Holmes, I am leaving tomorrow and did not get a chance to say goodbye or thank you. You have been such a positive, strong part in my stay here at Residence X11. Your passion, honesty and humbleness show through in all you do. I also thank you for sharing your story with us last week. I really connected with the journey and all that you have worked through to gain so many years of sobriety. Ms. Holmes again thank you for being part of my recovery journey.

Today my life is consumed with me serving others. Assisting others to restore their lives. Sharing my story to let others know that they too can heal from their past abuse and addictions. This feels the voids of what I have lost and gives me a since of purpose.

EPILOGUE

*W*riting my memoir took me about eight months because I was trying to articulate it in a way that no one would be offended. Then, finally, I gave myself permission to tell my truth not as a victim but as a narrator, author, and woman called by God to encourage and empower the hurting and dying so that they too can be free if they choose to believe.

I read somewhere that trauma is resolved if you are no longer troubled by it and your life is relatively free of a negative reaction to the event. Well, I found out that my trauma and life's events were not 100% resolved. There were moments when I felt nauseous, sad, angry, and most of all, some regrets. Thankful I was able to process my feelings and put the past in perspective and remind myself that my past does not define me, but it has assisted me in being an empathetic person who is well equipped to respond to the emotional states of individuals who too have suffered. My past has given me a burning desire to empower whoever will listen that they too shall overcome.

My hope for anyone reading this memoir is that you, too, can heal and find your personal resolution. Resolution means that your past fears do not control your life, and you're not disturbed when you remember the traumatic events. In other words, the traumatic event is remembered, but without the degree of emotional reaction that you felt before. It is simply an event that happened, part of your life story that you can share to empower others so they too can heal and be set free.

God's desire for us is to go and share our stories, whether we want to or not. God never wastes our pain. Only we do that. God has a plan for a great purpose and a beautiful future for all who believe in Him. Not despite our past, but because of it.

RESOURCES

For the addict still suffering I want to share this blog with you it is from Covenant Hills a Faith Based Treatment Center located in California.

God Is Still Here for You in Addiction. Addiction is like a black hole. It pulls in everything good and only leaves feelings of hopelessness and loneliness. Like a void growing larger and larger, the struggle of overcoming a substance use disorder can feel like an impossible task to achieve.

It is hard to say how your addiction grew to such proportions. It started as a recreational habit, helping you unwind after an exhausting day or loosen up in social circles. Over time, this seemingly harmless habit evolved into something darker and more sinister.

At this point, you may feel as if all hope is lost. The walls are closing in around you, leaving no options other than to perpetuate the vicious addictive cycle.

You might think that God has forsaken you, withdrawn all support and left you to fend for yourself. But this could not be further from the truth.

Psalm 50:15 reminds us that God asks us to call on Him in our times of trouble.

He promises to deliver us from the darkness of our sinful decisions and forgive our transgressions. All we need to do is ask and He will be there for us. Taking refuge in His loving embrace can be your greatest source of strength.

How to Overcome Addiction through God

God's love provides us the ability to overcome the most powerful addictions and achieve sustained sobriety and personal success. In turning to God to overcome your addiction, you must remember that:

God's Love is Amazing

While your addiction has made you feel worthless at times, you must remember that God sees through your faults and loves the person you are.

Psalm 46:1 reminds us that God is our shelter and strength, always there to help in times of trouble.

He does not expect his children to be perfect. He simply wants you to remain persistent toward overcoming your sins and constantly strive toward his everlasting love.

Learning to manage your addiction will take effort and sacrifice. It will require you to admit your shortcomings and push toward something stronger than yourself.

Holding on to God's hand during this storm can provide a stabilizing force capable of withstanding any temptation. You can do all things through Christ who strengthens you, including overcoming substance addiction.

God Wants Us to Experience Trials Because It is How We Grow

Learning to overcome difficult moments in life is the primary method we grow both emotionally and spiritually.

James 1:2-4 emphasizes this fact and reminds us to find joy in tumultuous life experiences.

It states: "Consider it pure joy, my brothers, whenever you face trials of many kinds, because you know that the testing of your faith develops perseverance. Perseverance must finish its work so that you may be mature and complete, not lacking anything."

Examples of God Helping Drug Addiction

Dealing with addiction can drain you of your strength and cause you to wonder what you have done to deserve such punishment. Fact is, God does not promise that you will never stumble and fall. On the contrary, He stresses that everyone will face trials and tribulations through those darkest hours. He will guide your steps with these promises:

2 Corinthians 12:9 – God tells you that his strength is all you need because His power is greatest when you are weak. When you are facing an addiction that makes you feel feeble and defeated, remember God is your strength and there to carry you through those moments.

Psalm 91:1-2 – God promises that when you run to Him for safety, He will protect you. He is your defender that can help you defeat all things, including the addiction, which have plagued you for so long.

John 15:4-5 – God is there to remind his children that their strength and power is derived from His strength and power. He states, "Remain in me, as I also remain in you. No branch can bear fruit by itself; it must remain in the vine. Neither can you bear fruit unless you remain in me." He does not care that we are all imperfect creatures. He embraces our faults and encourages everyone to use those faults to draw closer to him.

He promises to support his children and deliver them from all the obstacles that aim to defeat them.

Your addiction is an obstacle, not a brick wall. It is a bump in the road, not the end of your journey. God loves you no matter what you do, even through your addiction. Call out to Him and He shall be there for you.

You can conquer your addiction by handing control over to God. He loves you. He hears you. He will help you grow into the person you were born to be.

https://covenanthillstreatment.com/blog/
how-to-overcome-addiction-through-god/

TWELVE STEPS
AND BIBLICAL COMPARISONS

1. **We admitted we were powerless over our addictions and compulsive behaviors. That our lives had become unmanageable.**
    (Romans 7:18 "I know that nothing good lives in me, that is, in my sinful nature. For I have the desire to do what is good, but I cannot carry it out.")

2. **Came to believe that a power greater than ourselves could restore us to sanity.**
    (Philippians 2:13 "For it is God who works in you to will and to act according to his good purpose.")

3. **Made a decision to turn our will and our lives over to the care of God.**
    (Romans 12:1 "Therefore, I urge you, brothers, in view of God's mercy, to offer your bodies as living sacrifices, holy and pleasing to God–this is your spiritual act of worship.")

4. **Made a searching and fearless moral inventory of ourselves.**
   (Lamentations 3:40 "let us examine our ways and test them and let us return to the LORD.")

5. **Admitted to God, to ourselves, and to another human being, the exact nature of our wrongs.**
   (James 5:16a "Therefore confess your sins to each other and pray for each other so that you may be healed.")

6. **Were entirely ready to have God remove all these defects of character.**
   (James 4:10 "Humble yourselves before the Lord, and he will lift you up.")

7. **Humbly asked Him to remove all our shortcomings.**
   (1 John 1:9 "If we confess our sins, he is faithful and just and will forgive us our sins and purify us from all unrighteousness.")

8. **Made a list of all persons we had harmed and became willing to make amends to them all.**
   (Luke 6:31 "Do to others as you would have them do to you.")

9. **Made direct amends to such people whenever possible, except when to do so would injure them or others.**

(Matthew 5:23-24 "Therefore, if you are offering your gift at the altar and there remember that your brother has something against you, leave your gift there in front of the altar. First go and be reconciled to your brother; then come and offer your gift.")

10. **Continued to take personal inventory and when we were wrong, promptly admitted it.**
    (1 Corinthians 10:12 "So, if you think you are standing firm, be careful that you don't fall.")

11. **Sought through prayer and meditation to improve our conscious contact with God, praying only for knowledge of His will for us and power to carry that out.**
    (Colossians 3:16a "Let the Word of Christ dwell in you richly.")

12. **Having had a spiritual experience as the result of these steps, we tried to carry this message to others, and practice these principles in all our affairs.**
    (Galatians 6:1 'Brothers, if someone is caught in a sin, you who are spiritual should restore him gently. But watch yourself, or you also may be tempted.")

Celebrate Recovery, https://www.celebraterecovery.com/

REFERENCES

Bell, Carla. "Love in Action: A 'Golden Ticket' That Saved This Woman's Life." Pardon Our Interruption, http://www.muckrack.com/carlabell.

Celebrate Recovery. "Celebrate Recovery Home Page." Celebrate Recovery Homepage, Celebrate Recovery, 22 July 2021, https://www.celebraterecovery.com/.

"The Challenges of Prisoner Re-Entry into Society." SC-UMT, 21 May 2021, https://online.simmons.edu/blog/prisoner-reentry/.

Child Molesters: A Behavioral Analysis–Office of Justice Programs. https://www.ojp.gov/pdffiles1/Digitization/149252NCJRS.pdf.

"Childhood Trauma & Memory Loss." Integrative Life Center, 22 Apr. 2022, https://integrativelifecenter.com/wellness-blog/childhood-trauma-memory-loss.

"Crack Epidemic." Encyclopedia Britannica, Encyclopedia Britannica, Inc., https://www.britannica.com/topic/crack-epidemic.

"God Brings Us Suffering for Others' Sake." Desiring God, 30 June 2022, https://www.desiringgod.org/articles/god-brings-us-suffering-for-others-sake.

"God Is Still Here for You during Addiction." Covenant Hills Addiction Treatment Center, 30 June 2022, https://covenanthillstreatment.com/blog/how-to-overcome-addiction-through-god/.

Matthew Tull, PhD. "The Double-Edged Sword of Childhood Trauma and Dissociation." Verywell Mind, https://www.verywellmind.com/how-trauma-can-lead-to-dissociative-disorders-2797534.

"Self-Destructive Behavior." Wikipedia, Wikimedia Foundation, 4 Apr. 2022, https://en.wikipedia.org/wiki/Self-destructive_behavior.

"Signs of Codependency–What Addict & Codependent in Relationship Are Like." The Dawn Wellness Centre and Rehab Thailand, 14 June 2021, https://thedawnrehab.com/blog/telltale-signs-of-codependency/.

"NLT Life Recovery Bible, Second Edition"
Book by Arterburn M. Stephen and David A. Stoop

About The Author

Tammie Holmes is an ordained Chaplain Minister of the Gospel in Washington State. In 2006 Tammie truly surrendered her heart to Christ. Not long after God delivered her from a twenty-year crack addiction and mind-binding strongholds, this deliverance and intimate relationship with the Holy Spirit have given her passion for encouraging the hurting and dying. Tammie completed Chaplaincy training in 2008 and was ordained a minister the same year. Empowered by God's love, the Word, and the presence of the Holy Spirit, she has ministered to countless homeless individuals living on the streets in Washington. In 2013 Chaplain Tammie was invited to Lagos, Nigeria, for a 10-day Chaplaincy conference where she preached the gospel and prayed for the sick. Chaplain Tammie decided to go to college at the age of fifty. By 2016 She had a Counseling degree specializing in co-occurring disorders. "After

going through many battles, God has increased her anointing to encourage others to break the strongholds and yokes in their lives." Chaplain Tammie wanted to reach the community suffering from addiction, so she started "Revive Recovery, " a faith-based 12-step recovery group for women. In 2019, Chaplain Tammie did an unselfish act and donated a kidney to a stranger she met at a conference suffering kidney failure. Chaplain Tammie believes no matter what you have been through; you can conquer it and live the life God ordained for you. Today Chaplain Tammie works in with individuals struggling with Mental Health Disorders and the Disease of Addiction.

CPSIA information can be obtained
at www.ICGtesting.com
Printed in the USA
JSHW051912260822
29810JS00004B/13